Conducting a choir

CONDUCTING A CHOIR

a guide for amateurs

IMOGEN HOLST

London

Oxford University Press

New York   Toronto

Oxford University Press, Ely House, London W.1

GLASGOW NEW YORK TORONTO MELBOURNE WELLINGTON
CAPE TOWN IBADAN NAIROBI DAR ES SALAAM LUSAKA ADDIS ABABA
DELHI BOMBAY CALCUTTA MADRAS KARACHI LAHORE DACCA
KUALA LUMPUR SINGAPORE HONG KONG TOKYO

ISBN 0 19 313407 1

© *G & I Holst Ltd. 1973*

First published 1973
Second impression 1975

Printed in Great Britain by
Fletcher & Son Ltd, Norwich

Contents

CONTENTS

Acknowledgements

I wish to express my thanks to the following, who have kindly allowed me to reproduce copyright material: to Boosey and Hawkes Music Publishers Ltd. for extracts from Purcell's *Dido and Aeneas* (Exs. 46–58) and from Britten's *Rejoice in the Lamb* (Exs. 65–70), also for the note on 'Breathing' by Peter Pears from *The Book of the Dolmetsch Descant Recorder*; to Stainer and Bell Ltd. for 'Change then, for lo she changeth', 'Since first I saw your face', and 'Deo gratias' from *Invitation to Madrigals*, edited by Thurston Dart, also for 'This is the Truth', collected by Ralph Vaughan Williams; to the Oxford University Press for songs and rounds from *The Oxford Song Book*, Vol. II, edited by Thomas Wood (Exs. 2, 5, 12, 14, 32, 36), from *Singing for Pleasure*, edited by Imogen Holst (Exs. 7, 17–19, 24–5, 27–8, 31, 33, 35, 40–1), and from *Pammelia*, edited by Peter Warlock (Exs. 22, 29, 30, 34, 37, 39); to Faber Music Ltd. for Fig. XVc, and (for J. Curwen and Sons, Ltd.) for extracts from Handel's *L'Allegro* (Exs. 59–64); to Ascherberg, Hopwood & Crew, Ltd. for Ex. 21; and to the Performing Right Society, the National Federation of Music Societies, the British Federation of Music Festivals, and The Standing Conference for Amateur Music for extracts from their pamphlets.

I am also grateful to E. F. Ferry for information about the provision of music by public libraries; to the Rural Music Schools Association for the quotation about the two essential qualifications for amateur music-making in Chapter 11; to Rosamund Strode for the example of music copying in Fig. XIV; and to Dr John Agate for his approval of my suggestions for physical exercises in Chapter 9.

I. H.

Introduction

This book has been written for those who want to learn to conduct so that they can encourage people to sing choral music. 'Learning by doing' is the obvious way to find out what is needed, but the beginner can save a good deal of time at rehearsals, as well as avoiding unnecessary wear and tear, if he gets used to the feel of conducting before facing his choir. In the following pages Chapters 3 to 10 consist of technical exercises to be tried in solitude or, if possible, with other learners. From Chapter 11 onwards, the book is meant to be used as a supplementary guide to taking choir practices.

A guide-book to conducting can never be as sure of its immediate results as those instrumental Tutors where the author says to his reader: 'Cover the first hole with your forefinger and blow gently into the mouthpiece and you will get the note B.' There are no such infallible rules for conducting. It is true that there are recognized gestures for the various beats, and these can be taught. But the beats cannot produce the sounds. An inexperienced conductor may imagine that he is achieving the right choral effects by wildly waving his arms about, but if the members of his choir manage to sing well it will be in spite of his frantic gestures, not because of them.

On many occasions a conductor may be quite unnecessary. Singers in a choir, if they are familiar with the music, can hum the first chord, wait for a nod of the head from one of the tenors, and get on with it. And members of an orchestra who are used to working together can play a Mozart symphony without a conductor if they watch the leading violinist's bow at the start of a movement and at each pause and change of tempo, as instrumentalists did during Mozart's lifetime. It is only since the nineteenth century that an orchestral conductor, wielding a baton, has allowed himself to be transformed into an autocrat. Some of the famous conductors of today have acquired such glamorous reputations that audiences applaud them as if they were an entirely different sort of being from the players who actually make the music.

Any amateur choir-trainer who starts off by thinking that he is going to command power over others will be disappointed. He will find that he is the hard-worked servant of his singers, with no more glamour about his job than as if he were a teacher. Conducting is in many ways like teaching. The same virtues are needed: courage, patience, and sensitivity. If the beginner who wishes to be an amateur choir-trainer is an amateur in the true sense of the word and has a lasting passion for choral music, the only other qualifications he will need are a sense of rhythm and a good ear.

PART I

Basic essentials for a beginner

---

1. A good ear

Hearing and listening. An acute sense of hearing is an obvious necessity: no one who suffers from any sort of deafness should try to learn to conduct a choir. A 'good ear' for music involves listening as well as hearing, and listening means 'heedful hearing'. The most important part of a conductor's job is to listen to what he is hearing.

The mind's ear. In music, a great deal of listening has to go on in the mind's ear. This imaginary listening is just as much an everyday occupation as the silent process of remembering a telephone message or finding the words for the next sentence when writing a letter. And there is just as much need for accuracy and subtlety in the language of music as in the language of words.

Understanding the language of music. A conductor, like the producer of a play, must know what a work is about before he can direct it. Hearing a piece of music is not enough to enable a learner to discover how to conduct it: he has to become familiar with the language of music through singing or playing. Being able to make the right sounds is the best proof of a good ear: it is like speaking with the correct pronunciation and inflection when learning a foreign language.

Thinking how the written notes should sound. A choir-trainer has to be a good sight-reader. Many amateurs are content to learn their scores at the piano, but a conductor with a good ear should be able to imagine the sound of the written notes he is looking at. This may seem difficult in the early stages of learning conducting, but sight-reading always improves with intelligent practice, and the best way for a future choral conductor to practise it is to sing with other people, in choirs as well as in small groups with one voice to each part.

Recognizing the pitch. Some people, even when they are beginners, have 'perfect' pitch: they can immediately find the required level of sound for a note without any help. Do not feel too depressed if you have not got perfect pitch: it is sometimes a disadvantage, and it is not necessarily a sign of being a good musician. You will be able to develop your recognition of pitch by relating a given level of sound to any other note you hear or imagine. Carry a tuning-fork or a pitch-pipe in your pocket and try this out on suitable occasions. And listen critically to the intonation of any choir you happen to be singing in: it is easy to say 'that's out of tune', but a conductor has to recognize just how sharp or how flat it may be.

Self-criticism. Listening critically to one's own intonation is a much more difficult matter. A tape-recorder can be a help. If you find the ordeal of listening to the play-backs too painful, it would be advisable to have some singing lessons. There is no need for you to be a trained vocalist, but the phrases that you will eventually sing to your choir must be accurate and must sound convincing.

An ear for harmony. A knowledge of harmony can be an immense help to a choir-trainer. But it must be a practical experience of real harmony, not a theoretical acquaintance with textbook rules. If you are a pianist, try playing a Bach chorale every day: there are more than enough to last throughout the year. And then try transposing them to different keys. This is an excellent way of practising harmony and ear-training on music that one can never grow tired of. The old-fashioned method of listening to someone playing isolated chords on the piano as an ear-test is not so helpful. Music never stops still, and chords cannot make sense unless they are allowed to move on. A capacity for recognizing static levels of pitch is only of use to a future conductor if it can be combined with a sense of rhythm.

2. A sense of rhythm

Rhythm and flow. The word 'rhythm' is notoriously difficult to define. In the *Shorter Oxford English Dictionary*, the entry under 'rhythm in music' mentions 'the systematic grouping of notes according to their duration' and the 'kind of structure as determined by the arrangement of such groups'. But this information about musical grammar is only of limited interest. One of the non-musical definitions refers to 'functional movements, as of the heart', and this is of wider significance, because the heart's contraction and dilation can be compared to the tension and relaxation of the pulse in music. The dictionary's final entry under 'rhythm' says that it is 'related to flow'. Here at last is the word that comes nearest to describing the effortless continuity which is a basic essential in conducting. If you listen to an open-air performance of music in a garden on a day when the wind is blowing through the trees, you will notice that the trees 'keep time' throughout an andante $\frac{6}{8}$ and continue to keep equally good time when the music changes to an allegro $\frac{4}{4}$. It is this continual flow, linking days and nights and seasons, which miraculously enables a singer or player to slow down at a rallentando without destroying the pulse of the music.

Rhythmical and unrhythmical movements. There is no need for a conductor to be an athlete, but his gestures should have the purposeful ease of a good swimmer's movements. When an inexperienced swimmer is defeated by anxiety he loses his sense of rhythm: he stiffens and flounders, and goes under. A similar fate is in store for any inexperienced conductor who becomes over-anxious because he is not yet familiar with the music and is still uncertain what to do with his hands and arms. Practice is all that is needed.

Vitality in conducting. A purposeful ease in a conductor's technique will keep things going, but technique in itself is not enough to prevent the music from sounding dull. And dullness, alas, is a crime that professionals as well as amateurs can be guilty of. If you are feeling worried about whether you will be able to convey the vitality of the music you are going to conduct, you must not be led astray by people who declare that 'an exciting *personality* is what matters most'. A conductor does not have to be sensational: he has to be musical.

PART II

Learning how to convey the rhythm

---

3. Pulse and beat

The pulse of the music. One of the easiest ways to begin learning conducting is to start with a straightforward marching song, where the regular pulse of the music goes on and on. In songs such as 'This old man' (Ex. 1) and 'Bobby Shaftoe' (Ex. 2) the 'left, right' of the marching step matches the 'one, two' of the pulse of the tune.

Tension and relaxation. It is the balance of tension and relaxation in the continual 'left, right, left, right' that helps the marcher to keep going: each step takes over from the last, with a rhythmical give-and-take. The same give-and-take can be felt in the pulse of a marching song when the tune is sung or played with a rhythmical continuity.

The beat. A conductor's beat is the pulse of the music made visible.

Down and up. The beat for the 'one, two' of marching songs is 'down, up'. Try it, standing in front of a mirror and singing or imagining the tune of 'This old man' while beating time with your right forearm. (Left-handed readers will probably prefer to interpret 'right' as 'left' in these chapters.) If you beat 'down, up' with a stiff arm it will be the equivalent of walking with stiff legs: there will be no give-and-take, and each movement will need a new effort, which will soon become exhausting. Conducting needs a flexible movement for 'down, up' if it is to convey a pulse that is continuous. Learners often find it helpful to begin by holding the left hand loosely, palm upwards, at waist level; and then letting the relaxed right arm drop into it from a height: the weight of the right arm will make the left arm give way. Do this several times, noticing how both arms spring back to position at waist level. This is a flexible 'down'. If you had to lift the right arm up each time before dropping it for the relaxed 'down' it would be very tiring, so try the experiment of flinging it up with the left hand, letting it sail above your head. This is a flexible 'up'. Then try combining the two movements. The supporting left hand, having received the falling right arm and having sprung back to position, immediately flings it upwards, with the give-and-take of continuity. Practise this 'down, up, down, up' at the speed of a quick marching step. Now raise the supporting left hand to chest level, which is the right height for conducting. When you are used to this new level, try taking away the left hand, and let the right arm bounce back and spring up of its own accord. This 'down, up' is too wild and rough for conducting; make the movement smaller as you go on, until the beat is only three or four inches above the bouncing-back level at chest height. You will realize that there is a definite moment of arrival for the 'throb' of the pulse. If you can show this so that it looks confident and feels easy, you will *almost* be conducting. But the gesture will not yet be clear enough to carry messages from a conductor to his choir. To achieve this, it needs the help of a pointing finger to focus attention on the beat. (See Plate a.)

The hand as a sensitive indicator. The pointing finger in a choral conductor's beat is like the point of a stick in orchestral conducting. The finger must never be rigid. And it must never seem isolated from the rest of the arm, for rhythm is something that is felt through the whole of the body, even when it is indicated with a very small movement of the hand.

4. Starting and stopping

The preparatory beat. A conductor cannot expect the members of his choir to start a song together unless he shows them with a gesture when to come in. This gesture is the 'preparatory beat', which conductors make at the beginning of every piece of music, in order to draw sound out of silence. A preparatory beat must be at the same speed as the tune it is leading into. Although it is silent, it is part of the music, and it shares the same rhythmical continuity. It must not be too large and energetic, or it may interfere with the arrival of the first note. It should feel and look like a gesture of invitation, but it must be very precise, and the exact moment of the preparatory pulse must be clearly felt and shown. This needs a great deal of practice. In 'This old man' (Ex. 1) and 'Bobby Shaftoe' (Ex. 2) the preparatory beat is an up-beat, because both tunes begin on a down-beat. Try it in front of a mirror. (See Plate b.)

Ex. 1

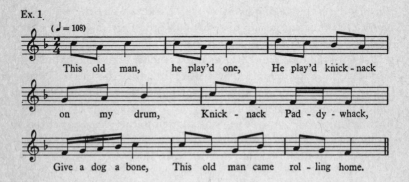

Ex. 2

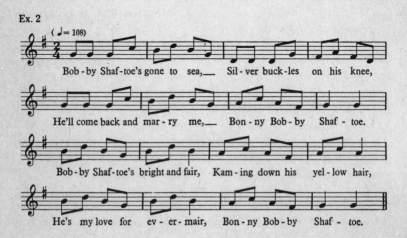

Holding an attitude while waiting to begin. Before making a preparatory beat, a conductor has to be sure that his singers or players are all watching him. He holds out his arm in an attitude of expectancy, and keeps quite still while he is waiting to begin. When you try this, be sure not to stiffen. Stand up straight and avoid hunching your shoulders: it is not until you can hold your arm in an easy attitude that you will be able to raise it in a rhythmical preparatory beat. Be careful not to move just before making the preparatory beat: any slight distraction could perplex the singers.

The moment of attack. In the early stages of practising conducting it is a great help to have a friend with whom you can experiment when trying to start a song such as 'Bobby Shaftoe' (Ex. 2). He need not be able to sing: a spoken 'Bob' will be enough for the vitally important moment of attack. You may find that you are making faces and mouthing the word 'Bob' to persuade him to come in at the right time. This is a frequent habit with choral conductors, and it sometimes helps in indicating subtleties of expression. But it should not be indulged in as a substitute for a clear beat. To prove to yourself that you can conduct without grimacing, take a newspaper in your left hand and hold it up to hide your face. Then try the preparatory beat again, with nothing but your right hand to rely on. If you can get the word 'Bob' to arrive at exactly the moment when you hoped to hear it, you will have learnt a valuable lesson, and you will be able to practise the following exercises in solitude, gaining a technique that will help you when you have a choir.

Two in a bar, beginning on the up-beat. 'The Noble Duke of York' (Ex. 3) is an example of a tune with two beats in a bar beginning on an up-beat. Here the preparatory beat will be a down-beat: but it must be a diminutive down-beat, as light as a feather. If it is heavy, the singers will either come in too soon, or they will let their breath escape just when they need it. The light-weight preparatory beat must, as always, indicate the throb of the pulse. And it must bounce. (Learners sometimes notice that professional conductors are apparently able to bring in a whole orchestra straight away on an up-beat: this is one of the differences between professional conducting and amateur conducting.)

Ex. 3

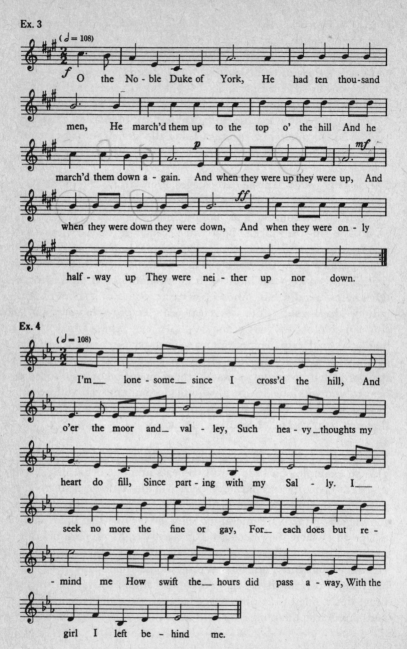

f O the No-ble Duke of York, He had ten thou-sand

men, He march'd them up to the top o' the hill And he

p

march'd them down a-gain. And when they were up they were up, And

mf

when they were down they were down, And when they were on-ly

ff

half-way up They were nei-ther up nor down.

Ex. 4

I'm___ lone-some___ since I cross'd the hill, And

o'er the moor and___ val-ley, Such hea-vy___thoughts my

heart do fill, Since part-ing with my Sal-ly. I___

seek no more the fine or gay, For___ each does but re-

-mind me How swift the___ hours did pass a-way, With the

girl I left be-hind me.

Two in a bar, beginning after the up-beat. Tunes with two beats in a bar very often begin *after* the up-beat as in 'The Girl I left behind me' (Ex. 4). Here the up-beat itself may not be helpful enough for a preparatory beat, because the tune begins half-way through it. An amateur choir should be given a very small down-beat as well as a medium-sized up-beat, so that the singers can know what the speed of the song is going to be. When you compare the start of Ex. 3 and the start of Ex. 4 you will realize that the up-beat in 'The Noble Duke of York' is more robust, because it is the actual moment of attack when the voices come in. Starting after a beat, as in 'The Girl I left behind me', needs much more practice.

Stopping at the end of a song. Starting and stopping are two of the things that beginners find most difficult. Stopping is easier than starting, for the singers will *have* to stop when the song is over. You will find that a marching song such as 'Bobby Shaftoe' (Ex. 2), which keeps the same speed to the end, will need no extra movement from the conductor to stop it after the last verse. Its final abrupt syllable will whisk into silence of its own accord, and you can leave your last beat up in the air.

Holding a final pause. There are some marching songs which can end on a pause. For instance, 'This old man' (Ex. 1) could have a long, sustained note for the final word 'home'. Try holding your hand out on the last up-beat with the palm upwards, as if you were holding the sound in it. Keep still for as long as the sound is to last, and then relax: you will find that your hand will 'drop' the sound quite naturally.

5. Appropriate beats for different time signatures

Three in a bar. Tunes with three beats in a bar are conducted 'down, out, up'. The 'out' moves *away* from the body: to the right side for a right-handed conductor as shown in Fig. I, and to the left side for a left-handed conductor. (If you have been doing it the wrong way you must be strong-minded enough to change to the correct way, otherwise your singers may feel as bewildered as if they were seeing a driver on the wrong side of the road.) The 'down, out, up' swings from 'one' to 'two' to 'three'. (See Fig. I.)

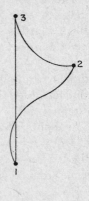

Fig. I

Ex. 5

Past three o' - clock, and a cold fros - ty morn - ing,

Past three o' - clock, Good mor-row, mas - ters all.

If you try beating this while imagining a tune such as 'Past three o'clock' (Ex. 5) you may find yourself drifting gracefully without showing the arrival at the pulse. As always, the throb of the pulse must be clearly indicated. Anyone watching your silent beats should be able to tap at precisely the right moment. Three-beat tunes which begin on the up-beat, such as 'Sweet Polly Oliver' (Ex. 6) will need a preparatory beat out at the side. This should be quite small.

Ex. 6

As sweet Pol - ly O - li - ver lay mus - ing in bed, A sud - den strange fan - cy came in - to her head; Nor fa - ther nor mo - ther_ shall_ make me false prove; I'll 'list for a sol - dier and fol - low my love.

Four in a bar. Tunes with four beats in a bar are conducted 'down, in, out, up'. The 'in' moves across the body: to the left side for a right-handed conductor, as shown in Fig. II, and to the right side for a left-handed conductor. Beginners often ask: 'Why is it wrong to do it the opposite way?' The answer is that in four-beat tunes the third beat is usually more important than the second, expecially when it is needed for a preparatory beat, and a movement out to the side will be more easily seen than a movement across the body. (See Fig. II. The curves in these diagrams are not meant to be exact. The shape of the loops may alter considerably, according to the different

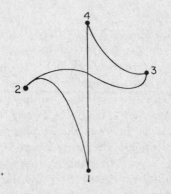

Fig. II

phrases of the music, but the direction of each beat should be followed as shown.)

If you try the beats in Fig. II to the tune of 'Never weather-beaten sail' (Ex. 7) you will find that it needs careful control to show the actual pulse at this slow speed.

Ex. 7 (♩ = 96)

Ne - ver wea - ther - beat - en sail more
Ne - ver tir - éd pil - grim's limbs af -

wil - ling bent to shore. Than my— wea - ry—
- fect - ed slum - ber more

sprite now longs to fly— out— of my troub - led—breast.

O come quick-ly, O come quick-ly, O come quick-ly,

sweet - est— Lord, and— take— my— soul to rest.

Indicating the difference between $\frac{2}{4}$ *and* $\frac{6}{8}$. There is a subtle difference between the 'down, up' of a $\frac{2}{4}$ tune and the 'down, up' of a $\frac{6}{8}$ tune. If you try conducting an imaginary choir in 'The Wassail Song' (Ex. 8) you will discover that it is possible to suggest the $\frac{6}{8}$ '*um*-cha, *um*-cha' for the words 'Here we come a-wassailing': the bouncing beats can be enlivened by a slight flick of the fingers for any quaver that follows a crotchet. At the $\frac{2}{4}$ chorus, the beat keeps to the same speed while the subtle indication of the time-pattern changes for the words 'Love and joy come to you'. In quicker $\frac{6}{8}$ tunes, such as 'I saw three ships' (Ex. 9), it might be too fussy to try and show the time-pattern with the hand: at the speed of ♩. = 120 the skipping rhythm should be felt but not seen.

Ex. 8 (♩. = 96)

1 Here we come a - was - sail - ing a - mong the leaves so
(2) be not dai - ly beg - gars etc.

green,_____ Here we come a wand - 'ring so

fair___ to be seen. Love and joy come to

you, And to you your was - sail too, And God

bless you and send___ you a hap - py new

year, And God send you a hap - py new year.___ 2 We

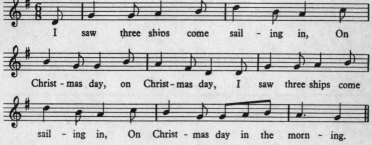

Ex. 9 (♩. = 120)

I saw three ships come sail - ing in, On

Christ - mas day, on Christ - mas day, I saw three ships come

sail - ing in, On Christ - mas day in the morn - ing.

Tunes that change the number of beats in a bar. In 'The truth sent from above' (Ex. 10) the time signature of $\frac{5}{4}$ alternates with $\frac{3}{2}$. The crotchets in a $\frac{5}{4}$ tune can be grouped in two different ways, either as 'one, two, THREE, four, five', or as 'one, two, three, FOUR, five'. The grouping of 'one, two, THREE, four, five' is conducted 'down, in, OUT, out, up'. (See Fig. III.)

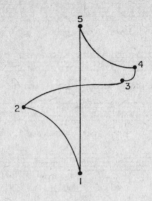

Fig. III

A tune that has its crotchets grouped as 'one, two, three, FOUR, five' is conducted 'down, in, in, OUT, up'. (See Fig. IV.)

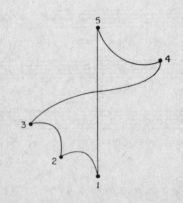

Fig. IV

Ex. 10

In 'The truth sent from above' (Ex. 10) the rhythmical shape of the song shows that the grouping is 'one, two, THREE, four, five', as in Fig. III. When the tune changes to $\frac{3}{2}$ there must be no interruption of the continuous flow of the music. The crotchet remains at the same speed, and the beat has to be transformed to six crotchets in a bar, grouped as 'ONE and TWO and THREE and'. This is conducted 'DOWN-down, OUT-out, UP-up'. (See Fig. V.)

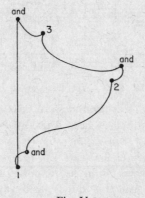

Fig. V

'*Divided*' *beats.* The 'and' of the 'ONE and TWO and THREE and' in Fig. V is called a 'divided' beat. It is a useful way of conducting tunes when the speed is too slow to be controlled with a single gesture for each main pulse.

6. Quick beats and slow beats

Very quick beats. In 'The Keel Row' (Ex. 11), the pulse is quicker than a marching song. At the speed of ♩ = 156 it is just possible to beat two in a bar, but the beats will have to be very small. You can prove this by trying it in front of a mirror: there is not enough time for the hand to travel more than about two inches up and down.

Ex. 11 Very quick (♩ = 156)

As I cam' thro' Sand - gate, thro' Sand - gate, thro'
Sand - gate, as I cam' thro' Sand - gate I
heard a las - sie sing: O weal __ may the
Keel row, the Keel row, the Keel __ row, O
weal __ may the Keel row that my __ laddie's in.

One in a bar. The speed of 'Bannocks o' bear-meal' (Ex. 12) is too quick to be conducted in crotchets. A useful way to test this is to try walking to the tune: if your walking step turns into running it means that the steps are too quick for beats. Ex. 12 has to be conducted 'one in a bar', with the dotted minim as the pulse of the tune. The 'one', as always, is 'down'. And this 'down', as always, will rebound. But instead of bouncing back to chest level and then making a beat in another direction, it continues to move upwards throughout the remainder of the bar, arriving at its highest point at exactly the right instant to allow the arm to drop swiftly downwards for the next 'one'. When you try this, you will discover that you have to let the weight of your arm fall freely, so that it can float up to the surface on its own momentum. It would be impossible to convey the lilting rhythm of Ex. 12 if you had to make an effort to drag your arm upwards at every bar.

Ex. 12

Slow 6/8 *tunes with six beats in a bar.* In 'Ye banks and braes' (Ex. 13) the speed is too slow for two beats in a bar. Learners would find it difficult to control the rhythm with such leisurely gestures. It is easier to conduct it in quavers. The six quavers are grouped as 'ONE, two, three, FOUR, five, six'. This is conducted 'DOWN-in-in, OUT-out-up'. (See Fig. VI, p. 20.)

Ex. 13

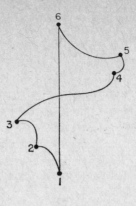

Fig. VI

Moderately slow ⁶⁄₈ *tunes with two unevenly divided beats in a bar*. The speed of ♩. = 60 in 'Blow the man down' (Ex. 14) is too quick to be conducted in quavers and too slow for two plain beats in a bar. It needs a more energetic version of the subtle indication of ⁶⁄₈ in Ex. 8. (See page 15.) This can be shown with an unevenly divided beat, 'DOWN-down, UP-up', in which the third and sixth quavers of the time-pattern rebound from the strong swing of the pulse. There is no need to keep this unevenly divided beat throughout the tune: at 'way-hay', a vigorous 'DOWN-UP' will be all that is wanted.

Ex. 14   **Moderate speed** (♩. = 60)

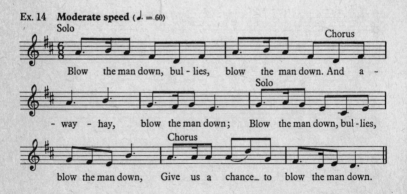

7. Suiting the style of the beat to the mood of the music

Marked beats and smooth beats. The speed of the crotchet beat in 'This old man' (Ex. 1) and in 'Sweet Polly Oliver' (Ex. 6) is the same, but the mood of the two tunes is quite different. In 'This old man', the beat is strongly marked and energetic: the arm moves swiftly and bounces back in a staccato manner, while keeping to the speed of ♩ = 108. In 'Sweet Polly Oliver', the beat is smooth and gracious: the arm takes as long as possible to move gently from the throb of one beat to the throb of the next, without losing control of the speed of ♩ = 108.

Loud and soft. A conductor's beat has to show whether the music is to be loud or soft. There are many different ways of doing this. One of the easiest ways is to make the beat larger when the music is to be loud, and smaller when it is to be soft. If you try this for 'The Noble Duke of York' (Ex. 3), following the dynamics that are shown, you will find that you have to give a very small second beat in the middle of bar 8, before the quiet entry of the voices. The second beat in bar 10 will be slightly larger, and in bar 12 it will be larger still. Most beginners make the mistake of relaxing the small beats for the quiet singing and working much too hard at the large beats when the music is loud. This is the opposite of what is wanted. Quiet singing needs strict concentration to prevent it sounding flabby: the conductor must help the singers by giving a precisely defined beat. Loud singing will look after itself in a straightforward song such as 'The Noble Duke of York': the *ff* beat, though large, can be relaxed.

Crescendo and diminuendo. The size of the beat will alter during a crescendo or a diminuendo. Try it on 'Bobby Shaftoe' (Ex. 2), beginning *pp*, working up to *ff* for the beginning of bar 9, and gradually getting softer until the last bar is *pp*. It will need a good deal of practice to control the speed, and you may not be able to realize that you are hurrying through the crescendo and dragging at the diminuendo. A metronome can be a help on these occasions, as it offers a crude, unbiased lesson in self-criticism.

Accelerando. An accelerando is one of the many things that is easier to practise on someone else. If you can persuade a friend to whistle or sing the tune for you, try conducting 'The Keel Row' (Ex. 11) with a gradual accelerando from bar 8 to the end. You will probably find your beat getting larger and larger in your efforts to get quicker and quicker. This will be frustrating, because the tune is too quick for a large beat, and your gestures may begin to look hysterical. What is needed is a very small staccato beat with tremendous determination behind it.

Rallentando. When practising a rallentando, try 'Ye banks and braes' (Ex. 13) with an expressive slowing down for the 'flowering thorn' in bar 12. A rallentando must never give the impression of putting on the brakes, for this will reduce the tune to a parody of itself. Avoid being emphatic about the quaver beats in bar 12, and aim at allowing the phrase to blossom and expand as if of its own free will. This will need a very legato gesture for the first three quavers of the bar. The word 'thorn' can have a slight pause, which means that there will be no indication of a fifth quaver in this bar. The pause should not feel static. Let your hand move calmly through it, to convey the flowing continuity of the tune. The *a tempo* at 'Thou mind'st me' needs a clearly defined beat to draw the pulse back to ♪ = 100, but you must resist the temptation to make your movements too large.

Subtle changes of expression in a song. The style of a beat often changes from one sentence to the next. For instance, in the chorus of 'Loch Lomond' (Ex. 15) there is a mood of determination in the sturdy dotted rhythm of the slow march at 'I'll tak' the high road', but in bar 5 the beat has to be smooth and expressive for the words 'I and my true love'. Singers in a choir, if left to themselves, might remain unaware of any change of mood: it is the conductor's responsibility to indicate these subtleties of expression.

Ex. 15 (♩ = 84)
Chorus

Then I'll tak' the high road and ye'll tak' the low, And

I'll be in Scot - land a - fore ye: But

I and my true love will ne - ver meet a - gain On the

bon - ny, bon - ny banks o' Loch Lo - mond.

8. Indicating the phrasing

The beat must show how each musical sentence should be phrased. Every
song has to be phrased according to its meaning, and a conductor's
gestures must help to convey that meaning. Nothing has a more
deadening effect on a performance than a time-keeper who goes
stolidly on from bar to bar with a heavy-handed beat that obstinately
adheres to the same size and the same stress without ever allowing
the tune to breathe. There is no need for a conductor to put in any
extra fussy movements: all that is needed is a sensitive response to
the shape of the music. In the songs quoted in the last few chapters,
the phrasing of each musical sentence is clearly implied in the words.
'I saw three ships' (Ex. 9) has its first two bars linked together; there
is a lift at the comma and a fresh emphasis for the repeated words 'On
Christmas day', and then the music of the last four bars moves on in
one phrase. The words of 'Past three o'clock' (Ex. 5) are just as
helpful. The comma after 'o'clock' tells the conductor that his
second beat in bars 2 and 6 will have a diminuendo lift and that
there will be a new beginning at the third beat. In bar 4, however,
the minim is phrased with a crescendo right through the smooth
second beat, and it is the third beat which has to be quiet and re-

laxed. If the conductor fails to show this in his gestures, the singers may forget to phrase according to the sense of the words, and the song will be wrecked by a falsely stressed 'mor-NING'.

Theoretical 'strong' beats. An unwanted accent on a weak syllable of a word is one of the most frequent faults in choral singing. It is often the result of a misunderstanding about 'strong' beats. An old-fashioned textbook rule says that 'the first note inside a bar is without exception accented'. This misleading statement is referring to the *pulse* of the music, and it does not mean that the beginning of each bar must be marked emphatically. It is true that the first beat of a bar is a 'main' pulse, which is theoretically a 'strong' beat. But there is no need for an *audible* stress or accent on the first beat of a bar unless the tune demands it. Ex. 7 would sound intolerable if it were sung 'NEV-er weather-BEA-ten sail'.

Words and music. 'Phrase the tune according to the meaning of the words' will always be helpful advice for a choir. But it would be a mistake to tell the singers to stress the words according to the *spoken* metre of the verse, because music transforms spoken words into something different. This applies even to traditional songs, where the words and the music seem to depend on each other for their very existence. In Ex. 10 (page 17) the word 'truth' in bar 1 and the word 'God' in bar 3 are both prolonged beyond their spoken length. As a result of this transformation the song can express far more than the spoken verse, if the singers phrase the tune musically.

Rubato. The traditional singer from Herefordshire who sang 'The truth sent from above' to Vaughan Williams in 1909 had no written notes in front of him and he was not concerned with time signatures or bar-lines. His phrasing was instinctive, and he sang with the sort of freedom that dictionaries describe as rubato. It is impossible to give singers or players any definite instructions about rubato. Composers can write an occasional *poco rall.* in places corresponding to the twelfth bar of 'Ye banks and braes'. But the rhythmical freedom which is essential in all music is something that a conductor has to go on discovering every day of his life. And in order to convey that freedom to his performers, he has to be able to move freely.

PART III

Exercises

---

9. Freedom of movement

Aiming at a supple strength. If you are an athlete or a dancer, leave out this chapter and go on to page 28. If you are already doing physical exercises every day, see if there are any additional arm movements mentioned here which might help you to gain a supple strength for conducting. If you never do any exercises and are not yet flexible in your movements, try the following suggestions, one at a time, for not more than five or ten minutes a day. When you get tired and your muscles begin to ache, relax by bending forward from the waist, letting your arms hang loosely with the fingers almost touching the floor: then come up *slowly*.

Finding a comfortable position for standing. A bad standing position can have an almost paralysing effect on a beginner's arm movements. You can prove this by standing with your feet apart and letting all your weight subside on to your heels: then give at the knees, hunch your shoulders, poke your head forwards, and stick out your chin; you will find that it is quite impossible to raise your arms freely. The difference is astonishing as soon as you stand up straight with your heels together and hold up your head without hunching your shoulders. Feel that you have an imaginary plumb-line from the back of your neck to the back of your heels. This imaginary cord is like a fishing-line: it hangs easily when at rest, yet at the first moment of tension it is strong enough to hold up the weight of the body. If you can feel this, you will be able to move as freely as you like when you are conducting: you can shift your weight from side to side, and step backwards or forwards on either foot, and move your head in any direction, and raise both arms, without losing the natural balance which can give you the right poise in everything you do.

Relaxing the muscles of the face and neck. Beginners often frown when they have to make an unfamiliar movement. The wrinkling of the forehead is connected with the stiffening of muscles in the face and neck. Try relaxing your jaw by allowing your mouth to hang open. (There is no need to look into the mirror for this exercise.) Now let your head flop forward with its weight hanging heavily: and *very* slowly roll it round, clockwise and counter-clockwise; once each way is enough. Then restore your head to its normal position, and let your lips come together again.

Using the left arm as well as the right. The following exercises should all be practised with both arms, one after the other. The left arm is needed in conducting, and its movements should eventually be just as agile as those of the right arm.

Freedom of the shoulders. Exercise I. Stand facing the north wall and swing your right arm freely from the shoulder, letting it move to and fro between the north-west and south-east corners of the room. For each 'to, fro, to, fro' count '1, 2, 3, 4': at the moment of counting, the arm should be at shoulder height and parallel to the floor. Do this several times without a break. Then vary it, starting 'to, fro, to' as before, but swinging through a complete counter-clockwise circle for '4'. Continue 'fro, to, fro' for the next '1, 2, 3,' making a complete clockwise circle for '4'. Do this several times without a break, and then repeat the whole exercise with the left arm, swinging north-east and south-west. Exercise II. Point to the north-west with your right forefinger and slowly draw a complete clockwise circle with your whole arm. Continue this circling movement, keeping to the same slow speed and always using the whole arm, but gradually letting the circle get smaller and smaller. By the time the circle is no bigger than a wedding ring you should be pointing north-east. Now reverse the movement, beginning with a very small counter-clockwise circle and gradually increasing the size until your largest circle is once more pointing north-west. Repeat this with the left arm, beginning by pointing north-east.

Exercises for the forearm. Exercise III. Hold up your right arm at shoulder level and support it above the elbow by allowing the weight of the upper arm to rest on the palm of your left hand. Then swing your forearm in gentle clockwise circles (north-east and south-west). Relax, and then do it circling counter-clockwise. Now try again without the supporting hand. Repeat with the left arm (north-west and south-east). Exercise IV. Hold your unsupported right arm as in Exercise III and begin the clockwise circling as before, but let it get gradually smaller and smaller: then unwind counter-clockwise, increasing the size of the circle. Watch your upper arm, and keep it as still as possible, without stiffening anywhere. Repeat with the left arm.

Exercises for the wrist. Exercise V. Support your right forearm by allowing its weight to rest on the palm of your left hand. Then move your wrist in small circles, clockwise and counter-clockwise, keeping the forearm as still as you can, and not letting the elbow drop with the weight of the upper arm. Your fingers should remain relaxed. Then try the exercise again, without the supporting hand. Repeat with the left wrist. Exercise VI. Stand with both arms hanging down quite freely. Shake both wrists as quickly as you can, letting your hands flap. If your arms are as relaxed as they should be, they will also be shaking, right up to the shoulder. As a second part of this exercise, try raising your arms gradually to shoulder level at each side, and then let them gradually sink down again, while continuing the shaking movement all the time.

Finger technique. Exercise VII. Hold out your right arm at chest level in the 'attitude while waiting to begin' that was mentioned on page 9. Support your wrist in the palm of your left hand and move your forefinger in fairly slow, small circles, clockwise and counter-clockwise. Let your other fingers hang limp: they should not move in sympathy with the forefinger. Watch your thumb: if it bends, or rears up, it is a sign of stiffening. When you can manage the exercise, take away the supporting hand. Repeat with the left forefinger. Instrumentalists and typists have plenty of opportunity for acquiring a finger technique, but if you find that your fingers are inclined to be weak and clumsy, try resting your hand on a table and then raising and lowering each finger in turn.

Independent arm movements. A conductor has to be able to use both arms independently, with, for instance, a quick energetic right-hand beat going on at the same time as a slow sustained gesture for the left arm. Some of the exercises suggested in this chapter could be combined for practising independent arm movements. Try the very slow circling in Exercise II with your right arm, simultaneously with the quicker wrist-circling in Exercise V for your left hand. And then try the circling in Exercise VII with the left forefinger, while the right arm practises the second part of Exercise VI. You may find yourself getting rigid in your efforts to concentrate: guard against clenching your teeth and tightening your knees and screwing up your toes. Always relax between exercises.

10. Practising various gestures needed in conducting

Learning to beat with the left hand. A conductor should be able to use his left hand to convey anything that he wants. Practise the beats mentioned in Chapters 4, 5, and 6 with your left arm, using your left forefinger as the indicator. Remember that the gesture for 'out' will be to the left, away from your body, and the gesture for 'in' will be to the right, across your body. (See pages 11–13.) Try beating each time signature in front of a mirror, aiming at an easy movement that should look just as confident as a right-hand beat.

Conducting with both arms simultaneously. There are a good many occasions when it can be helpful to beat with both arms at once: for instance, at the beginning of a work, at a change from quick to slow or from loud to soft, at a rallentando, or at the climax of the music. When you try beating with both arms you will realize that the gestures for 'in' and 'out' will be moving in opposite directions. For large or medium-sized beats you must hold your arms further apart than the width of your shoulders, or you may find your two hands colliding with each other at the movement for 'in'. Practise this in a moderate $\frac{4}{4}$, and also in a slow divided-beat $\frac{4}{4}$: 'DOWN-down, IN-in, OUT-out, UP-up.'

Occasional use of the left arm for special indications. Learners sometimes feel more secure if they keep both arms moving all the time. This is seldom necessary in choral conducting unless the choir is very large. With a small group of singers it is better to keep the left arm in reserve for special occasions, such as a sudden dramatic entry of the men's voices after they have had several bars rest. As an exercise for this, try beating three bars of andante $\frac{3}{4}$, making the first two beats of the first bar *f* and all the remaining beats *p*: use both arms for the two *f* beats and the right arm only for the *p* beats. Beginners, when faced with this exercise, often ask: 'What do I do with my left arm when it's not wanted?' You should let it drift down quite naturally until it is hanging at your side: meanwhile, you should be concentrating your attention on your right-hand beat. Avoid holding your unemployed left arm at chest level, with the hand tightly clenched. This can have an unnerving effect on a choir, for it is a sign that the conductor is tense.

Changing the level and the position of the beat. The entries of the different voices in choral singing need a beat that is flexible enough to adapt itself to a change of level and a change of position. Fig. VII shows a fairly usual grouping of singers on a platform, with the tenors and basses standing at least two feet higher than the sopranos and altos.

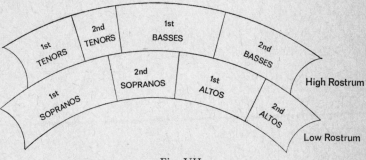

Fig. VII

If you had to conduct the choir in Fig. VII in a quietly flowing $\frac{3}{4}$ chorus with the 2nd altos beginning alone and the 1st tenors coming in a bar later, your preparatory beat for the tenors would have to travel through an arc of 120° without jerking itself away from the sustained andante. This needs practice. A useful exercise is to stand facing a blank wall and imagine that the figures of a huge clock-face are drawn on it. Begin beating an andante $\frac{3}{4}$ at 'six o'clock' and then move on, a bar at a time, through seven and eight, right round the circle, keeping your beat smooth and continuous. Then try moving to and fro from nine to one to eleven to four, and from three to ten to two to eight. Practise this with various time signatures, including $\frac{5}{4}$ with alternate groupings of 'down, in, OUT, out, up' and 'down, in, in, OUT, up'. If you can do this exercise easily, with the left arm as well as with the right, you will have achieved considerable freedom of movement. Whether you can use this technique to control the rhythm of the music you are going to conduct is something that you will only find out when you have a choir to work with.

PART IV

Forming a choir

---

11.   Finding the singers

Taking over an existing choir from another conductor. If you are asked to take charge of a choir that has lost its usual conductor there will be obvious advantages in accepting the invitation: the singers will be used to each other; the different voices will be reasonably well balanced; there will be a regular evening set aside for practices each week and a suitable meeting-place for them; and the choir will already have a repertoire of part-songs, with copies to sing from. All this will save you a good deal of trouble, but there may be disadvantages. The previous conductor may have had ideas about music that were very different from your own, and the choir may be urging you to perform works that you hate in a style of singing that you consider deplorable. (This sometimes happens to professional choir-trainers, who may have to spend at least half a year persuading their singers to unlearn most of what they have learnt.) Even when the previous conductor has been an admirable musician it is not always an advantage for a beginner to start by taking over an existing choir: he may find that the singers can get on perfectly well without him, and this will deprive him of the painful but necessary experience of learning by trial and error.

Starting with a small group of beginners. If you have the courage to begin on beginners who want to sing part-songs but have never belonged to a choir, you will have to be prepared to work with a very small group for the first few weeks or months. It is possible to start with only three singers. If they are sufficiently enthusiastic about the music you choose for them and the way you encourage them to sing, there will soon be other people asking if they may join them.

The necessary qualifications for a choir member. Your singers should be genuinely eager to practise choral music together. And they should have the two essential qualifications for amateur music-making: the desire to learn and the willingness to work.

Auditions. When forming a choir it is as well to begin by hearing each singer separately. Conducting a weekly choir practice is very different from conducting an occasional sing-song where a crowd of people, many of whom have never sung before in their lives, can achieve astonishingly good results in some of the rounds quoted in Chapter 12. At a 'drop-in-and-sing', everyone is welcome and individual shortcomings are obliterated. Sing-songs, however, are ephemeral. Choir practices occur over and over again, and individual defects can be blatantly evident. Any weakness that is tolerated at an audition must be of a sort that is curable.

Growlers. 'Monotones', or 'growlers', who are unable to control the pitch of their voices, are not easily cured. With children, all that is needed is a skilful, patient teacher. (My father used to say that he could cure anyone under the age of ten if he could give them a five-minute lesson every day: I still have one of his scribbled lists with the names of the schoolchildren he helped in this way at the time when he was writing *The Planets*.) Grown-up growlers are much more difficult to cure. They are quite likely to be keen music-lovers, and on occasions they have been smuggled into large choral societies, where they have sung among the basses without doing appreciable damage. But a growler in a very small group of singers would be a burden to himself as well as to others: he should be encouraged to learn an instrument and to join an amateur orchestra or a brass band. Growlers are in a different category from the basses who find even moderately high notes so uncomfortable that they prefer to drop down an octave in the naïve belief that it will not be noticed. This weakness can fairly easily be cured by the unyielding persistence of the conductor and the friendly co-operation of the other basses. (In forty years' experience of taking sing-songs I have only once been utterly defeated in a struggle with an *8va* bass: he was a distinguished ex-Chancellor of the Exchequer who sang *two* octaves below his neighbours.)

The soprano who fancies herself as a soloist. A singer to beware of in a small choir is the soprano who, having failed to get the leading part in the local operatic society, turns up at a choir practice without asking for an audition, saying that she 'doesn't mind coming along occasionally to help'. She should be avoided, not just because of the steely edge to her voice (a technical problem which will be referred to in Chapters 14 and 15) but chiefly because she lacks the essential qualifications mentioned above in the third paragraph.

Choosing suitable music for a choir of mixed voices without any balance of parts. In the early stages of forming a choir of mixed voices you will probably have too few men. If there are basses but no tenors you will be able to discover suitable part-songs for three voices, such as Ex. 43. (See page 65.) If you have a fair number of sopranos and altos, one tenor, and no basses, as I did in my first amateur choir, you may find that one of the easiest ways to solve the problem is to begin with rounds and canons.

12. Teaching rounds

Learning by ear. There can be many advantages in beginning by teaching rounds: the singers will be learning by ear and will therefore be looking at the beat instead of burying their heads in their copies: their singing will warm up straight away instead of being strangled by the doubts of the non-sight-readers: everyone will be learning the tune simultaneously instead of waiting for each section to grapple with the notes in turn: they will welcome the necessary repetition of a phrase while they are learning it, and they will have the satisfaction of singing music that is worth while, however simple it may be.

Rounds and canons. The main difference between a round and a canon is that in a round the second voice enters when the first voice has reached the end of a phrase in the words, while in a canon the second voice can come in much sooner, when the first voice is still in the middle of a phrase. Rounds and canons can end with all the voices pausing simultaneously on the last note of a phrase; or they can be sung right through to the final note, in which case the latest group to enter will be left singing alone at the end. It is usual for rounds to end on a combined pause and for canons to be sung right through, but there is no rule about it. In the examples in this chapter the pauses in brackets refer to the last time only: the asterisks show where each new group is to come in.

Division of voices. Rounds and canons often have a wide compass, and it is therefore advisable when dividing up the singers to mix the sopranos and altos, and to mix the tenors and basses, so that there are high and low voices in each group. This will make it possible for altos and basses to leave out any notes that are too high for them, while sopranos and tenors can sing lightly when the notes are low.

Placing the singers. If you have only a small group of singers it is better to put them in a semicircle rather than in several short rows. Let them sit while they are learning the notes by ear: they can stand up to sing if they want to.

Some practical advice on conducting rounds and canons. Learn the tune by heart very thoroughly before you conduct it: you should be able to imagine the sound of the combined voices in your mind's ear. When you teach a round or canon to your choir, choose a key that suits your own singers, transposing any example in this chapter up or down if necessary. Sing it to them straight through at the right speed, and then teach it phrase by phrase: keep each sentence very rhythmical, even if it has to be slightly slower to start with; and link each repetition so that the sound has a continuous pattern. When the singers have learnt the tune securely in unison, divide them into groups and show them where each group will be coming in: you will find that a canon usually sounds best if the men's voices are left to the last group, though this does not always apply to a round. Tell the choir how many times you will be doing it in parts: a short canon, if sung with varied dynamics, can go on for at least half a dozen times, and the singers will find it easier to count on their fingers than to try to remember how far they have reached. Always begin a canon with everyone singing it in unison as an introduction: this establishes the shape of the tune and offers a reminder to the whole choir, and it gives confidence to the singers in the first group when they are able to go straight on with the canon in parts. Look at each group in turn while bringing them in with a preparatory beat. In canons that are sung right through to the final note you will have to use your left hand for stopping each group, one after another, while you continue conducting the remaining voices; the left-hand gesture must be phrased with the music to prevent it looking like an abrupt dismissal. In rounds, there will be no need to have the whole tune sung in unison as an introduction: the first group can come in straight away. Three times through is usually enough for a round. You will have to plan the stopping-place to suit the spacing of the last chord: for instance, in 'Come, follow' (Ex. 26) it would be a mistake to have the men's voices ending high up on the 'greenwood tree': they should arrive for their final pause at the last note of the first line. You will also need to plan the dynamics of a round: Ex. 26 could be sung *mf* the first time through, *p* the second time, and *f* for the third time, with a crescendo and rallentando to lead into the pause.

Two warnings which will apply on any occasion, whatever the music may be. DON'T TAP WITH YOUR FOOT while you are beating time, and DON'T SING while your choir is singing.

Suggested examples of rounds and canons on which an inexperienced conductor can learn by trial and error.

'The swan sings' (Ex. 16). As legato as possible.

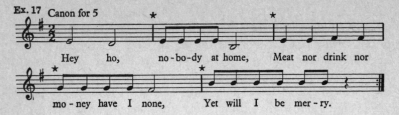

Ex. 17 Canon for 5

'Hey ho, nobody at home' (Ex. 17). This rhythm needs enthusiastic words: let the singers exaggerate the rolled 'r' in 'drink'.

Ex. 18 Round for 4

'Humming Round' (Ex. 18). Teach it to them with each note sung to 'la', and when they know the tune, get them to hum it with loose lips that almost fall apart. You will probably hear them sniffing at the end of each line as they snatch a breath: if so, you should help them to discover that there is always time to relax before breathing.

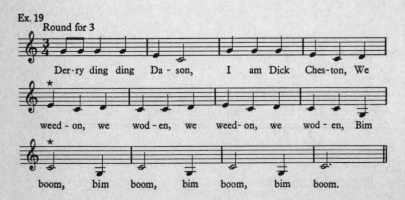

Ex. 19 Round for 3

'Derry ding ding' (Ex. 19). Persuade the singers to hum on the 'm' of 'boom'. At the end, the third group of voices can have a very long pause on the last note, with the hum getting fainter and fainter, so that it seems to reverberate in the distance.

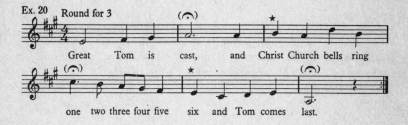

'Great Tom is cast' (Ex. 20). If some of the singers already know this round they may possibly become careless about the rhythm of the quavers. Encourage them to pronounce the 'two three four five' very distinctly: clear words will always help to cure ragged rhythm.

'Who will ferry me?' (Ex. 21). The repeated word 'over' should have a crescendo to the beginning of the last bar, and then a diminuendo. This will prevent the repetition from sounding dull and static: it will also help the intonation.

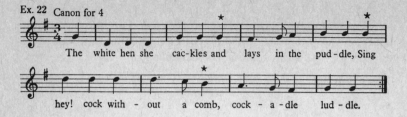

Ex. 22 Canon for 4

The white hen she cac-kles and lays in the pud -dle, Sing
hey! cock with - out a comb, cock - a -dle lud - dle.

'The white hen' (Ex. 22). Sing it to them up to time and then teach it slowly, getting gradually quicker until your beat changes from three in a bar to one in a bar. The rhythmical attack will be improved if the singers pronounce the 'h' in 'white'.

Ex. 23 Round for 4

Ah, poor bird, Take thy flight
Far a - bove the sor - rows of this dark night.

'Ah, poor bird' (Ex. 23). As smooth as possible. At 'this dark night', avoid a hissing sound on the 's': it is the only consonant that can always be heard clearly in a sung phrase, without any additional help from the singers.

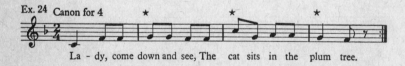

Ex. 24 Canon for 4

La - dy, come down and see, The cat sits in the plum tree.

'Lady, come down' (Ex. 24). Having sung it to them very quickly and lightly, begin teaching it slowly, loudly and firmly. When you gradually increase the speed, changing from two in a bar to one in a bar, you must try and make it quieter and lighter. The singers will

38

probably get louder and louder in their effort to get quicker: this will make you want to stamp and shout, but you will have to resist the temptation and try to control the speed and dynamics with a neat, precise movement of the hand. If the choir can manage to sing it in parts, *ppp*, at ♩ = 108, it will seem like a miracle to all concerned, and it will prove to you that *the music itself can take charge* if the notes have been thoroughly practised and if the conductor does nothing to get in the way of the rhythm.

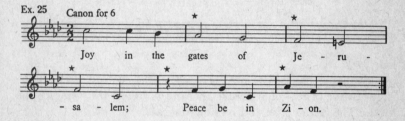

'Joy in the gates' (Ex. 25). The anonymous composer of this beautiful canon wrote it without bar-lines: the beat must be phrased according to the words.

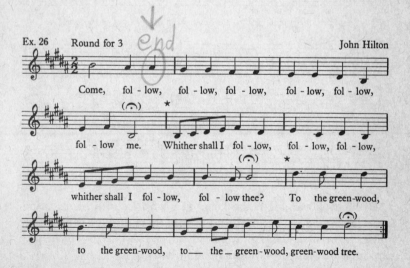

'Come, follow' (Ex. 26). The two crotchets of the repeated 'follow' must not be equally stressed, or the tune will sound heavy and plodding. A springing beat, the equivalent of a jaunty step, will help the singers to tongue the 'll' flexibly and to toss the second syllable lightly aside.

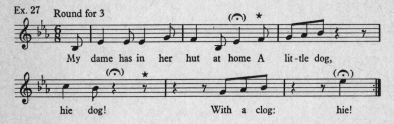

'My dame has in her hut' (Ex. 27). The silences must not be static: your beat should enable the singers to feel the swing of the pulse. The last note should be sung staccato.

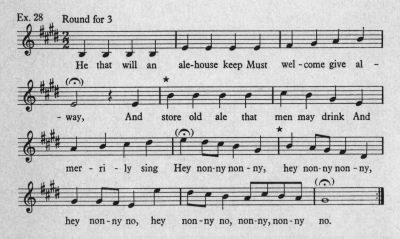

'He that will an ale-house keep' (Ex. 28). Let the men's voices begin this round, and plan the number of times through so that they finish on the first line. An accent at the end of bar 10 will help to banish an unwanted first-beat stress in bar 11.

Ex. 29

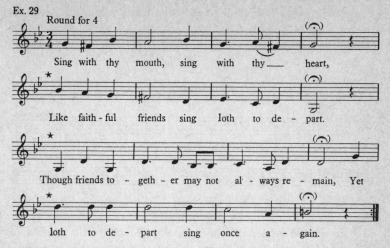

Sing with thy mouth, sing with thy____ heart,

Like faith-ful friends sing loth to de - part.

Though friends to - geth - er may not al· - ways re - main, Yet

loth to de - part sing once a - gain.

'Loth to depart' (Ex. 29). This sad song should not sound dismal: *warmth* is what is needed.

Ex. 30

Hey ho, to the green - wood now let us

go, Sing heave and____ ho. And there will we

find both buck and doe. Sing heave and__ ho. The hart, the

hind and the lit -tle pret - ty roe. Sing heave and____

ho. Hey ho, to the ho. Hey ho, hey ho!

'Hey ho, to the greenwood' (Ex. 30). Encourage the altos and basses to get louder at 'Sing heave and ho', as the notes are low for

41

sopranos and tenors. When teaching the tune in unison, be sure that they phrase bar 5 according to the words, but keep to your three beats in the bar.

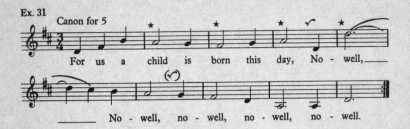

'For us a child is born this day' (Ex. 31). Teach it with three beats in a bar and then, when they are singing in parts, change to a slow one in a bar: this will help the sustained flow of the music. If you have a fair number of singers you can do it in ten parts instead of five.

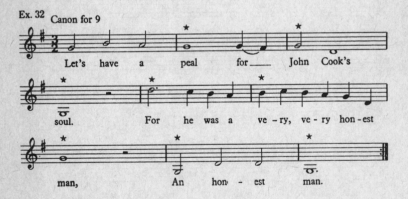

'Let's have a peal' (Ex. 32). This canon needs a fairly large choir: it is not suitable for one voice to a part, owing to its large compass.

'Sumer is icumen in' (Ex. 33). The Ground can be sung by men's voices in two parts as a continuous foundation to the main canon; it can begin before the first entry of the words 'Sumer is icumen in', and can go on for several times after the last 'ne swik thou naver nu'. The dynamics of the round should be varied: it sounds well if sung *f* for the first time with a gradual diminuendo throughout the repeat, ending *pp* as if in the distance.

Ex. 33

Ex. 34

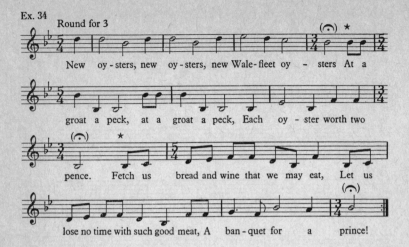

'New oysters' (Ex. 34). Teach them the tune up to time, phrase by phrase. It would be too jerky with five beats in a bar at for instance ♩ = 136: the tune needs an unevenly divided beat, with a longer up-beat in the bars phrased 2 + 3, and a longer down-beat in the bars phrased 3 + 2. Practise this uneven beat in solitude until it swings easily, and be aware of the words that are phrased across the bar-line in bars 3–4, 8–9 and 9–10. If the singers can get the feeling that $\frac{5}{4}$ is an easy rhythm it will save them a good deal of frustration when they have to sight-read twentieth-century choral music.

PART V

Improving the singing

13. The well-being of the choir

A satisfactory meeting-place. For reasons of economy a newly founded choir may decide to meet for weekly practices at the house of one of the singers. This can have its drawbacks. The room may be too warm for hard work: the upholstered armchairs and sofas may be too large for the singers to be able to get near to each other and too low for them to be able to sit up when singing: and the thickness of the carpet and curtains may muffle the sound of the voices. As an alternative, the choir might decide to meet in a church. Here the over-resonance could have a flattering effect on the voices, and this would be an encouragement. The singers could certainly sit up straight on the hard pews, but they would have to remain in fixed rows, one behind the other. And the lofty building might be so cold in winter that people would probably begin to croak after the first few minutes. It is worth paying a small rent for the use of a club-room or similar meeting-place, where the temperature can be adjusted and where the upright chairs can be placed in a semicircle. When arranging the room, you should avoid putting the singers in a position where they would be facing an unshaded electric light or a window.

Fresh air. If possible, the practice-room should have a window that opens. Lack of air can transform willing, intelligent choir members into sullen slackers who sing flat. Never allow anyone in the room to smoke at any time during a practice, for the air the singers breathe is the raw material of their singing. A practice-room without any windows must be air-conditioned.

The problem of noise. Air-conditioning can seem very noisy when one is trying to concentrate on listening. Even strip-lighting can produce a wheezy version of the chord of the dominant-minor-ninth which insinuates itself between the end of one phrase and the beginning of the next. The noise of traffic can be a much worse problem, and in the difficult choice between having some fresh air and having comparative quiet you may be forced to compromise by opening the window for the first song and closing it for the second. Never put up with the intruding sound of a radio during a choir practice: any other discomfort would be preferable to the ordeal of trying to get used to it.

Dealing with discontented singers. There will certainly be singers in your choir who are dissatisfied. You may have to face the usual problem of individuals who cannot get on together. And there may be other less obvious causes of discontent, such as unpunctuality. A conductor must be unfailingly punctual himself, and he must insist that everyone else is ready to begin on time. Another reason for dissatisfaction is one that choirs are seldom able to do anything about: they may have a conductor who wastes time at rehearsals by explaining the beauties of the music at great length instead of getting on with the singing. A golden rule for all conductors is DON'T TALK TOO MUCH.

How long should the weekly practice last? An hour's rehearsal is long enough for a small choir of local singers. For a larger choir, in which some of the members have come from a distance, it is better to go on for an hour and a half. If the singers ask for a quarter of an hour for coffee-drinking, persuade them to wait until the practice is over.

14. Correcting the faults

Listening to what you are hearing while imagining what you hope to hear. When listening critically to the sounds that are coming from your choir you must not allow their imperfections to absorb your whole attention so that you forget to follow the shape of the music that is in your mind's ear. Nor must you let yourself be so carried away by the excitement of what you hope to hear that you lose interest in the sounds that are actually going on.

Criticizing the singing. When you have launched the singers into a song, let them reach the end of it if they can. It is frustrating for a choir to be stopped after the first few bars and told about a mistake. There are one or two glaring faults, such as 'scooping' from just below the pitch of the note, or slithering down sentimentally (as in the 'sorrow' of Ex. 23) which damage the music so unbearably that they should be rooted out immediately they occur. These are faults of self-indulgence. Other faults, which may be the result of the singers' inexperience, can wait until the end of the song before they are pointed out and corrected. You will have to remember every detail that needs to be improved, while you are still conducting. When they have stopped singing, mention each point and help them to correct it: they should start at the beginning of a phrase so that the flow of the music can carry them over their difficulty. After every fault has been worked at, let them sing the song straight through for the satisfaction of joining it together again, and then tell them that it is better. If it is obviously just as bad as before, you can at any rate say 'it's *going* to be better' before asking them to make another attempt at improving any of the details. You should never apologize for having to do the same difficult passage over and over again: choirs flourish on hard work. Never ask them to repeat anything without saying why you want it again: aimless repetition is always depressing. (Professionals can suffer from this during recording sessions when, after a long silence, the disembodied voice of a talk-back from the far-off balance-room suddenly says: 'Again, please.' It is no use being told to try again unless one knows what one is trying for.)

Getting flat. When the singers are out of tune, do not shout 'you're getting flat' while they are still struggling in the middle of a phrase, as it will only make matters worse. Sing them the the passage, or play it on an instrument, so that they have a pattern of sound to imitate. Show them how an interval may need special care to avoid flattening: there is an example at the end of 'Loth to depart' (Ex. 29) where the major third of the final cadence is higher than most of them may want to make it. The end of the second bar of 'Who will ferry me?' (Ex. 21) is another example of a perilous interval: it is a large step up for the word 'river', and the diminuendo for the weak syllable must not be allowed to flatten the last note.

Getting sharp. When a choir sings sharp it is often the result of forcing the tone during a crescendo on a rising phrase, as in the last two bars of 'Come, follow' (Ex. 26). The hard-edged voice of one determined singer can drive all the others a semitone sharp against their will. Be careful that your beat does not whip up the choir into a state of over-excitement: you should help them to relax when singing loudly, as suggested in the second paragraph of Chapter 7. (See page 21.)

Hurrying and dragging. Over-familiarity with a song can make singers careless about hurrying, as in the quavers in 'Great Tom is cast' (Ex. 20) mentioned on page 37. Another frequent cause of hurrying is the singers' agitation when trying to get a difficult passage right. For instance, the quavers in 'New oysters' (Ex. 34) at 'Fetch us bread and wine' can scramble themselves into 'Fe'sh-bre'n-wye' if the conductor fails to insist on clear rhythmical words. In the next bar of 'New oysters' there is a danger that the difficulty of articulating 'Let us lose no time' could make the singers slow down: they should be persuaded to practise the quavers lightly as well as clearly. In slow songs it is possible that the singers may take too long over a new breath at the beginning of each sentence, and they may be inclined to indulge in a rallentando where it is not wanted. A good exercise for curing these two faults is the eight-part canon 'Praise God from whom all blessings flow' (Ex. 35). If the singers are used to this as a hymn in church they may have got into the habit of waiting for the organist at the beginning of each line, and they will almost certainly want to slow down at the end of each verse. Curing bad habits is one of the most difficult tasks in conducting. If you can control the counterpoint of Ex. 35 with a smooth expressive beat you will have learnt to apply some of the technique you have practised in solitude. And the singers, during their first attempt at this eight-part canon, may have discovered that dragging can result in the total breakdown of the music.

Lazy vowel sounds. Out-of-tune or unrhythmical singing is often caused by careless pronunciation of the words. Vowels can sound muddy and meaningless when the singers are too lazy to open their mouths. A useful cure for the 'refained' type of singing is Ex. 36, where the travesty of 'Mai daime heth a laime, taime craieen' will soon be defeated by the rhythmical energy of the tune: the singers will have to make such an effort to pronounce the tongue-twisting consonants in the third line that they will be compelled to open their mouths.

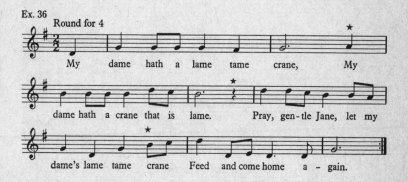

Slack consonants. Flabby lips and languid tongues need the discipline of quick, exaggerated consonants in a tongue-twister such as 'Kit and

Tom' (Ex. 37). Let the singers practise *whispering* the words, up to time, before they attempt to sing it. 'Fie, nay prithee John' (Ex. 38) is another helpful exercise for rapid, clear articulation. Here the difficulty of managing the tongue-twister is combined with the challenge of having to place each interval accurately. Try teaching them the second and third lines to 'la' at a gentle allegretto before working it up to a robust allegro with the words.

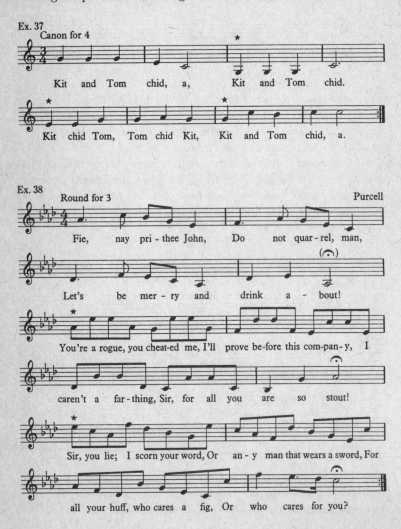

Ex. 37

Canon for 4

Kit and Tom chid, a, Kit and Tom chid.

Kit chid Tom, Tom chid Kit, Kit and Tom chid, a.

Ex. 38

Round for 3

Purcell

Fie, nay pri - thee John, Do not quar - rel, man,

Let's be mer - ry and drink a - bout!

You're a rogue, you cheat-ed me, I'll prove be-fore this com-pan-y, I

caren't a far-thing, Sir, for all you are so stout!

Sir, you lie; I scorn your word, Or an - y man that wears a sword, For

all your huff, who cares a fig, Or who cares for you?

Difficult notes. There are some intervals which choirs find difficult to imagine clearly when they are trying to memorize a pattern of sound. The ninth bar of Ex. 28 (see page 40) looks easy enough on paper, but when you first teach it to your singers they may stumble over it. This will be because they are not yet aware of the underlying harmonies which you already have in your mind's ear. It will help them if you play the tonic chord throughout bar 8, the dominant seventh in bar 9, and the tonic again in bar 10: they will then recognize that the interval which had once seemed difficult is now an expected sound. Other notes which may at first be troublesome to find are the diminished or augmented intervals in minor tunes. For instance, the first bar of 'Loth to depart' (Ex. 29) may seem awkward. Avoid practising the F♯ to B♭ as an isolated difficulty: let them feel the shape of the tune by singing the opening phrase with a stepwise ascending triplet from the F♯: then, having once bridged the gap, they will be able to manage the interval quite easily.

High notes. When singers are scared of high notes they close up the back of their throats and the result is a squawk of protest. Help them by giving a relaxed and confident gesture of invitation at the approach of a high note: fright is infectious, and you should never permit yourself to look as anxious as you may be feeling. Practise 'Farewell, mine own sweetheart' (Ex. 39) in unison, beginning with the sopranos and tenors as written, and then taking it through again a fourth lower for the altos and basses. The last bar should be as smooth as possible, and there will be no need for them to exaggerate the consonants. Clear pronunciation is something that may have to be sacrificed in a high sustained phrase, but they must always sing the words as if they meant them.

Ex. 39

Avoiding a dreary sound. 'Adieu, sweet Amaryllis' (Ex. 40) can sound dreary if the mournful words are sung with a pale grey tone. As in 'Loth to depart' (Ex. 29), the singers need to feel that they have a mellow warmth in their voices.

Ex. 40   Round for 3

A - dieu, sweet A - ma - ryl - lis,   For   since to   part your

will   is,   A - dieu, sweet A   —   ma   ryl -

- lis.   O   woe - ful_____   ti -

- ding!   There is   for   me   no   bi   —   —   —

- ding.   Yet   once a - gain e'er that   I   part   from

you,   A   —   ma - ryl - lis,   sweet,—   A - dieu.

15. Aiming at a better sound

Good tone. Good voices are rare, and if you are lucky enough to have one in your choir you will find that its benign influence will help to convert any soprano who shrieks, or alto who booms, or tenor who bleats, or bass who bellows. It will also help to encourage those husky, faint-hearted singers who may previously have been too reticent to let themselves be heard. If you are unlucky, and all the members of your choir sound inadequate at first, you should realize that their tone is bound to improve, and that it will go on improving, because they will be getting accustomed to singing in the right way.

This is what matters most in voice-training, and you should encourage them to practise the music you are teaching them for at least five minutes every day.

Breathing. The most helpful lesson I have ever had about breathing was from Peter Pears, who gave the following advice: 'Never lift the shoulders when you breathe: you will soon lose your breath. Rather expand the middle of the back. Breath must be stored and its output controlled; this must be done by the muscles in the very centre of the body. Breathe quickly and deeply; for practice, sniff in and out: quick in and slow out; slow in and quick out, but *always deeply*. The chest is not deep enough. Store your breath below and behind the chest, as it were in a barrel, and hold it in the barrel till the last drop is gone!' I have noticed that when he gives auditions to amateur singers he often has to criticize them for wasting their breath by letting it escape, instead of turning it all into sound. Recently I asked him whether a choir-trainer should spend any time on breathing exercises, and he told me that with his own pupils he says as little as possible about breathing and lets them learn on the songs they are singing.

Vocal exercises. The conventional scale up or down to 'Ah' is not the most helpful of exercises because it is so often heedlessly skimped through as a perfunctory concession to so-called 'technique'. If you want to ask your choir to do vocal exercises, try a fairly slow scale, coming down, to the words 'Full fathom five thy father lies', and let them sing through each smooth consonant. (Be careful not to let them turn the first word into 'Foo-erll': this is a fault which even professional singers can be guilty of.) Another helpful exercise is to sing a fairly quick scale, going up, to the repeated word 'Allelluia, alleluia'.

The pure vowel sounds in Latin. The five Latin vowel sounds, 'ah, ay, ee, oh, oo', are purer than English diphthongs, and they are therefore a help when aiming at a better tone. The beautiful 'Sanctus' (Ex. 41) can bring out the best in an amateur choir. (The most suitable order for the voices to enter is Soprano I, Alto, Tenor, Soprano II, Bass: this will give the right spacing for the final cadence.)

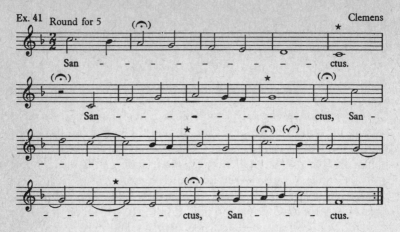

Byrd's 'Non nobis' (Ex. 42) is another masterpiece which can transform a group of inexperienced singers into a very much better choir than they thought they were.

PART VI

Sight-reading

16. Notation

Singers who pretend to be able to read. Large choral societies sometimes accept singers who have never learnt to sight-read, on the tacit understanding that they should sit next to experienced readers and imitate the sounds they hear. These non-readers become so skilled at following, a tenth of a second late, that they give the impression of singing from the printed copy and, as a result, the habit is tolerated. In a small group of singers it is not so easy to pretend to be able to read. When there are only two second sopranos and the one who can sight-read is unable to get to a rehearsal, the other one will be reduced to an embarrassed silence. If you want your singers to do unaccompanied choral music you will have to face the task of teaching them to read. They will try to resist the suggestion, partly because they think the written symbols of music are incomprehensible mysteries, but chiefly because they feel secretly ashamed of their ignorance. You should reassure them by telling them that learning the musical alphabet is like learning the Russian alphabet: all that matters is that one should have a good reason for beginning and a good chance of regular practice.

Testing each member of the choir. It is worth giving up the whole of one rehearsal to testing each individual's sight-reading, with the rest of the singers waiting their turn in another room. Choose several test pieces and change them frequently during the session so that the singers who are waiting are not influenced by the sounds they hear. An unaccompanied sight-reading test should be very short and easy, and it should have a satisfying tune that the singers are not likely to know. Play the chord of the piece and the first note of the tune: allow about two minutes for looking at it, and then repeat the chord and the note. Singers whose teeth are chattering with nerves should be given a second chance. If they want to, they can sing it first to 'la', then repeat it with the words. Those who fail should come for a quarter of an hour's combined sight-singing practice every week.

Gaps in the choir's knowledge of rudiments. When you are teaching the non-readers every week you must realize that many of them will know very little about the rudiments of music: signs and symbols such as ♭ ♯ ♮ or :‖ │ ɪ │ and │ 2 │ may mean nothing to them. And you must be prepared for some muddled misunderstandings that will have been left over from previous lessons of long ago: they may say that they had been told to 'count three whenever there is a dot after a note', which can be disastrous in sight-reading dotted minims in $\frac{6}{8}$. Encourage them to ask questions if they are puzzled. And teach them one thing at a time, beginning with the *sound*.

Tonic sol-fa: for and against. The great advantage of the tonic sol-fa system is that it helps a sight-reader to recognize the importance of the tonic in its relation to all the other notes in a tune, whatever the key may be. Its chief disadvantage is that it destroys this feeling for the tonic whenever the tune is in the minor: for example, in 'Ah, poor bird' (Ex. 23), having admitted that the key is C minor, it insists on labelling the first three notes 'lah te doh'. Another drawback is its peremptory way of asserting fixed definitions throughout a passage of subtle enharmonic modulation. No system of musical notation can be infallible, because the living language is always adapting itself to changing needs. Whatever method you choose for teaching your beginners, you will have to be prepared to be flexible.

Alphabetical names of the notes. The first seven letters of the alphabet are familiar enough to set any beginner's mind at rest. But your non-readers should not accept them as written symbols until they have recognized the sounds they represent. Let them each get a pitch-pipe tuned to A: it will cost them no more than the price of two Sunday newspapers. (They can use it at the start of their daily practice mentioned on page 53.) Sing them the notes A B C, giving each note its alphabetical name, and let them imitate the sounds. It will be easy for them to practise the remaining letter-names on something they have already been singing, such as the scale up to 'Alleluia, alleluia' (see page 53). Let them sing it first to 'Alleluia' and then to 'C D E F G A B C'.

Tones and semitones. The 'Alleluia' phrase is a good example for teaching them about tones and semitones: when they sing it to the alphabetical names of the notes they will be able to feel and hear the meaning of 'E to F is a semitone and B to C is a semitone', instead of having to accept the information as a sentence from a textbook. The descending scale to 'Full fathom five thy father lies' mentioned on page 53, when sung to C B A G F E D C, will help them to recognize the falling semitones. It will also enable them to get used to the letter-names in the reverse order.

The octave. When practising the letter-names to the scale of C going up and coming down, choose a rhythm such as $\frac{4}{4}$ crotchets beginning on an up-beat, so that the exercise makes musical sense. Then let them sing the octave from the lower C to the higher C several times, in the same rhythm. Point out to them that the tenors and basses sing their scale an octave lower than the sopranos and altos, and that the lowest note of the women's scale is the same level of pitch as the highest note of the men's scale. Tell them that this is 'middle C'.

Staff notation. Teaching staff notation to a group of non-readers becomes much easier if you can have the use of a blackboard or a sheet of paper with large staves. If your choir meets in a schoolroom, there may be a music blackboard available: if not, you can buy a small canvas sheet, marked with four staves, that rolls up and is easy to carry. (For 'equipment', see page 153 under 'Useful Information'.) Write Fig. VIII and Fig. IX and tell the singers that the symbol represents the sound of the note C and that the stave can be used for writing any other notes.

Fig. VIII

Sopranos and Altos — Middle C

Fig. IX

Tenors and Basses — Middle C

Then write Fig. X and let the sopranos and altos sing the notes to their letter-names.

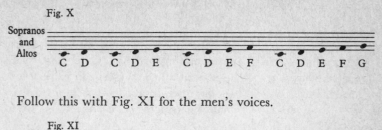

Fig. X

Sopranos
and
Altos

C D C D E C D E F C D E F G

Follow this with Fig. XI for the men's voices.

Fig. XI

Tenors
and
Basses

C B C B A C B A G C B A G F

Let the singers realize that although the lines of the stave are drawn an equal distance apart, the distance in sound is not always equal, because of the semitone between E and F and between B and C.

Clefs. Your beginners will notice that the stave needs some sort of sign as a clue to whether it is meant to be used for sopranos and altos or for tenors and basses. Tell them that the clue is a sign called a 'clef' and that it is written on one of the five lines to indicate a definite level of pitch. Show them how the highest note in Fig. X, the G above middle C, is the level chosen for the 'treble clef' for sopranos and altos (see Fig. XII). The lowest note in Fig. XI, the F below middle C, is the level of the 'bass clef' for tenors and basses (see Fig. XIII).

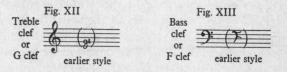

Treble
clef
or
G clef

Fig. XII

earlier style

Bass
clef
or
F clef

Fig. XIII

earlier style

(It is helpful to show the earlier forms of the clefs, so that the singers can see that the modern signs are elaborate versions of a G and an F: most beginners are unaware of the connection.) You can now write an ascending and descending scale of C in the treble clef for the sopranos and altos to sing to the letter-names, followed by a descending and ascending scale in the bass clef for the men: both scales will be starting from the familiar security of middle C, and the singers can feel confident in reading the three new notes that were not written in Fig. X and Fig. XI.

Melodic intervals. Write the ascending scale of C in both clefs, aligned one above the other, so that all the singers can work simultaneously. Practise each melodic interval above C, beginning with the stepwise notes 'C D E' and then singing 'C E', and so on, up to the octave.

Time-patterns and time signatures. 'Keeping time' can be the most difficult part of learning to sight-read. Let your beginners start with something familiar, such as 'The swan sings' (Ex. 16), which they can sing by ear in unison, giving each note its letter-name. Encourage them to beat time with one hand while singing it. Then write out the tune for them, in both clefs, one above the other, and let them look at its written appearance as they sing it. They will then be able to learn the unfamiliar names for the things that already feel and sound familiar: 'crotchets', 'quavers', 'triplets', 'minims', 'three crotchets in a bar', 'up-beat', and 'repeat'. Try 'Derry ding ding' (Ex. 19) in the same way: the new things to learn will be the two quavers as the normal division of the crotchet, the leger lines for the low G, and the dot after the final note which makes it last for one and a half times its normal length. Then try 'Sumer is i-cumen in' (Ex. 33) with the tenors and basses singing the tune as well as the sopranos and altos. They will already know the feel of the skipping rhythm, so there is no reason for them to be bewildered by the written appearance of six quavers in a bar: they can learn about the figure 8 representing a quaver in the time signature, and about the dotted crotchet as the pulse of the tune. They can also learn to recognize the crotchet and quaver rests. And they will realize that there is no need for a '3' above the quavers in the second bar. The difference between $\frac{6}{8}$ and $\frac{2}{4}$ often puzzles beginners, so it would be as well to write out 'The Wassail Song' (Ex. 8) and let them sing it while beating two in a bar: they will be able to learn the meaning of the duplet, the time signature $\frac{2}{4}$, the dotted quaver and semiquaver in bar 15, and the tied note in the last bar.

Keys. Instead of teaching key signatures as a series of written state-ments, let them discover the need for sharps and flats from their own practical experience. Give them 'The white hen' (Ex. 22) starting on middle C, and they will agree that the opening is too low for comfort. Transpose it to F, but without any key signature, writing one note at a time and asking them to sing it, note by note, with the letter-names. When they get to the second note in bar 6 they will probably call it 'B' while singing B♭. Let them hear a B♮ and they will immediately learn the need for a B♭. Write the key signature of F, explaining that it is a trouble-saving device to show that every B is a B♭, at whatever octave it occurs, throughout the piece of music. Then go back to 'The white hen' and write it in G in the same way, so that they learn the need for an F♯.

Recognizing the written appearance of familiar tunes. The following tunes will give your beginners a new key signature every week, and there will be several new details of notation for them to learn. Add some appropriate dynamics, including the 'hairpin' signs for cresc. and dim. And suggest to the singers that they might each have a manu-script notebook and write out the key signatures and time signatures and any other information that they want to be reminded of.

MAJOR KEYS: sharps
'Let's have a peal' (Ex. 32) G major, $\frac{3}{2}$, (semibreve, minim rests)
'For us a child is born' (Ex. 31) D major, (slur and tie)
'Great Tom is cast' (Ex. 20) A major, $\frac{4}{4}$
'He that will an ale-house keep' (Ex. 28) E major, $\frac{2}{2}$
'Come, follow' (Ex. 26) B major

MAJOR KEYS: flats
'Sanctus' (Ex. 41) F major
'Hey ho, to the Greenwood' (Ex. 30) B♭ major (1st and 2nd time bars)
'My dame has in her hut' (Ex. 27) E♭ major (grouping of rests)
'Fie, nay prithee John' (Ex. 38) A♭ major

MINOR KEYS: modal
'Humming Round' (Ex. 18) A minor, modal
'Hey ho, nobody at home' (Ex. 17) E minor, modal
'Who will ferry me?' (Ex. 21) D minor, modal

MINOR KEYS: sharps

'Farewell, mine own sweet-heart' (Ex. 39) B minor (accidental: mention that it only applies at that particular octave, and that it lasts for the rest of the bar)

'Adieu, sweet Amaryllis' (Ex. 40) F♯ minor, (♮, the 'warning' accidental in bar 13, compared with the essential 'contradicting' accidental in bar 18)

MINOR KEYS: flats

'Loth to depart' (Ex. 29) G minor

'Ah, poor bird' (Ex. 23) C minor

'Joy in the gates' (Ex. 25) F minor

17. Practising sight-singing

From the known to the unknown. The suggestions in the last chapter were meant for non-readers who were discovering about rudiments and notation through the familiar music which they had already learnt by ear and had sung by heart. Real sight-reading begins when the music is unfamiliar. Your learners who are practising for the first quarter of an hour of every rehearsal will need some suitable unknown tunes that are worth singing and that are not too difficult. 'The Folk-Song Sight Singing Series' is the best collection I know. (See page 152 for details.) These small books contain nearly seven hundred folk tunes from countries throughout the world, and although they were intended to be sung to the tonic sol-fa names of the notes they are just as suitable for sight-reading to the syllable 'la'. The tunes, which are excellent, are all very short. Your singers should always repeat each song. Encourage them to go on if they make a mistake, for they may be able to right themselves before they get to the end. Sight-singing should *always* be rhythmical: it is even more important to keep time than to sing the right notes.

Taking turns to sight-read individually. When your singers are getting used to sight-reading in unison you should persuade them to take it in turns to sing individually. The folk-songs mentioned in the last paragraph are phrased with slurs according to the musical sentences in each tune, which makes it easy for the singers to hand on the song to each other, phrase by phrase. After the first agonizing struggles of solo sight-singing they will gain confidence when they find that they can manage without having anyone else to rely on. And they can all learn from each other's mistakes, as well as from their own.

Learning both the F clef and the G clef. Unfortunately the tunes in the 'Folk-Song Sight Singing Series' are all in the treble clef: there are very few unison sight-reading exercises published in the bass clef. (See page 152.) Singers in a choir should know both clefs. Your tenors will be obliged to learn to sing equally well in either clef, because they will be reading in the bass clef in short score and in the treble clef, an octave lower, when the music is written in open score. The other members of the choir would find it a great advantage to know both the F clef and the G clef for singing choral music: they would not only be able to get their leads from the other voices more easily, but they would also be able to follow the music more intelligently during the passages when they were not singing.

PART VII

Unaccompanied choral music

---

18. Madrigals

Madrigals as chamber music. As soon as your choir members can sight-read, you will be able to give them madrigals to sing. It is worth remembering that madrigals were never intended to be conducted as choral music. They were meant for individuals who sat round a table and sang from single voice-parts that were printed without bar-lines: one of the singers probably indicated the pulse with a slight movement of the hand. This was true chamber music, with the singers leaning towards each other and listening to the contrapuntal entries in close imitation. Madrigals sound best when they are sung with only one voice to a part, but they can give a great deal of pleasure to singers in a choir.

Balletts. The easiest madrigals to begin on are the short balletts in three, four, or five parts, with all the voices moving together in a cheerful, dancing rhythm. In the three-part 'Change then, for lo she changeth' (Ex. 43) the tenors can sing with the basses if they take the low notes very lightly.

Singing from printed copies. If your choir is large enough for a semi-circle of two or three rows, be sure that the singers in the back row can see the beat when they stand up: a conductor should have a clear view of all the singers' mouths as well as their eyes. While they are sitting down to learn the notes they will almost certainly want to rest their copies on their laps. You must firmly prevent them from doing this, before they get into the bad habit of putting their heads down when they are singing. Show them how to hold their copies at the right level for watching the beat. They will need to be told not to fold one page behind the other, but to have two pages spread out at once, which saves time in turning over. Singers should always bring pencils to a rehearsal, to write reminders of what has been asked for, to add any extra dynamics, and to mark in the beats in any passage where the time-pattern is complicated. It can also be helpful to write an arrow in the margins of an open score as a quick guide to the right stave to look at.

Ex. 43

William Holborne (1597)

The first attempt at part-singing. Members of a choir often have difficulty in hearing each other until they are used to singing together in parts. And at first they may grudge the fact that they cannot even hear their own voices: if so, you should assure them that no individual voice is meant to be heard above the others in a well-balanced group of singers. When they have learnt to listen to the other parts they should be able to avoid singing too loudly. Madrigals seldom need much volume of tone: their dynamics are relative, and a triumphant climax, such as the 'fa la la' at the end of Ex. 43, will owe its excitement to the energy of its rhythm. (The vowel should not be heavy as in 'lard' but light as in 'lull'.) When beginning to work at Ex. 43, ask them to read the words to themselves and to look at the key signature and the time signature. Then let them hum the first chord, forming it from the lowest note upwards. If there are experienced sight-readers in the choir, try it straight through in parts, even if some of the singers get lost at the first attempt. Then work at each part in turn: you will find that all the voice-parts in a madrigal have real tunes which stand any amount of repetition.

Cross-rhythms. Bars 4–5 and bars 12–13 in Ex. 43 have the characteristic hemiolia cross-rhythm, that is, two $\frac{3}{4}$ bars linked together almost as if they were one bar of $\frac{3}{2}$. This cross-rhythm is subtle: the altos are whole-heartedly in $\frac{3}{2}$, while the other voices hint at its possibility. It would be a mistake to change your beat to $\frac{3}{2}$, because the music would lose the slight pull against the pulse which has enlivened so many cadences from medieval times until now.

Madrigal singing without a conductor. When the singers have worked hard at Ex. 43, aiming at clear words and varied dynamics, they may find that they know it by heart without having set out to memorize it. Try the experiment of starting them off and then leaving them to get to the end without a conductor. They will possibly sing better than they have ever sung before.

Building up a repertoire. There are enough superb madrigals to last a choir for a lifetime. If you start each practice by singing an exhilarating ballett it will warm up the voices as if by magic. It is a good plan to build up a repertoire of short madrigals which the choir can sing by heart, at a moment's notice, on any appropriate occasion.

19.   Part-songs

The difference between a madrigal and a part-song. In a madrigal, the voices are all equally important, and the tune is often handed from one to another, in imitation. In a part-song, the tune is nearly always in the highest voice, with the others singing an accompaniment.

Learning each part with the bass as the foundation. When teaching a part-song, always begin with the tune, so that the singers can know what they are going to accompany. In 'Since first I saw your face' (Ex. 44) the compass of the tune is suitable for all the voices to sing it through in unison. The bass part, which is the foundation of the harmony, is second in importance to the tune and should be practised next. While the basses are singing it, the others can follow their own parts and silently whisper the words in rhythm. Then let the tenors sing their line, while the basses repeat their part very quietly. Next, the altos can sing out, while the tenors and basses sing their parts *pp*: this way of getting to know the notes is a help to those who have only recently learnt to sight-read, as it enables them to hear their own part above the supporting harmonies. When the sopranos join in, the three lower voices should be able to feel that they are accompanying them. Even in the early stages it is important to aim at the right balance of parts. The editor of Ex. 44 has marked the dynamics with this balance in mind: although the sopranos are given the same gradation as the other voices, they should always sound more prominent. The basses can have a real *f* in bar 5, where they sing the tune in imitation. In bar 9 the altos should be quieter than the tenors and basses, but they can enjoy a crescendo in bar 11.

Breathing-places. The singers should avoid taking a new breath where it interferes with the meaning of the words. A comma in a sentence can always provide a suitable breathing-place if it is needed. When a sentence has the sort of comma that is not wanted for a new breath, there should be a clear articulation at the beginning of the following word: for instance, at the first double-bar in Ex. 44 the words 'What, I' must not sound like 'Wha-tye'. This is a fault that can always be cured if the singers remember to pronounce their words as if they meant them. The word 'and', when it suggests that there might have been a comma just before it, can often be used as a breathing-place,

but it needs intelligent phrasing to avoid a sudden burst of sound
from newly re-filled lungs. A new breath after a word that ends in a
consonant such as b, ck, d, g, p, s, or t can result in untidy phrasing if
the singers are haphazard about it. For example, in bar 10 of Ex. 44
the altos, tenors and basses should not pronounce the 'st' of 'fast'
whenever they like. It should sound on the fourth crotchet of the
bar. Help them to sing it gently by avoiding a jerky beat.

Ex. 44

Thomas Ford (1607)

2. The sun, whose beams most glorious are, rejecteth no beholder,
   And your sweet beauty past compare made my poor eyes the bolder;
   Where beauty moves and wit delights, and signs of kindness bind me,
   There, O there, where e'er I go, I leave my heart behind me.

Fitting in the words of a second verse. Part-songs sometimes have the words of the second verse printed separately from the notes, as in Ex. 44. Let the sopranos sing the second verse alone while the others follow their own parts, glancing to and fro: this will make it easier for them to attempt the new words. Some of them may insist on writing the second verse under the notes: others, who are used to singing hymns in church, may find it quite easy. If the basses, in their agitation at looking both ways, should sing 'be-hol-DER' for their rising fourth in bar 4, you must be lenient with them the first time it happens, as they have probably got too much to think of at that moment. But this distressing fault, which is so often a sign of absent-mindedness, should be ruthlessly dealt with in music that has already been practised.

Joins between verses. The silence between verses in a part-song must never give the impression that the sound has been switched off: this produces a tense gap in the music, with everyone waiting for something to happen. Inexperienced conductors sometimes beat out a solemn 'ONE TWO THREE' before the second verse of Ex. 44, but this is unnecessary and unhelpful. The silence should feel like a pause in a rubato: it is part of the continuous flow of the rhythm. Stand still and feel relaxed, and listen to the silence: then bring in the singers on the up-beat without further preparation, as they will already know the speed of the tune.

20. Anthems and motets

The difference between an anthem and a motet. Anthems have English words: motets are usually in Latin. Although anthems and motets were written to be sung in church, amateur choirs enjoy working at them during their ordinary practices.

Avoiding the faults of the wrong sort of church choir. If you have members
of a church choir among your singers you may possibly find that
although they can sing 'He that will an ale-house keep' in a natural,
warm-hearted tone of voice, as soon as they are faced with the words
'Lord have mercy' they immediately sound spineless and sancti-
monious. This will only occur if they are unfortunate enough to
belong to the wrong sort of church choir where 'Amen' becomes
'Awmern', and 'Oh God' is pronounced 'Er Gud'. Lazy vowels are
partly to blame, but most of the damage is due to the mistaken
notion that it is respectful to sound depressed in church. The best
cure is to get them to work at a glowing motet such as 'Deo gratias'
(Ex. 45, p. 72) which can be sung either in its original Latin or in an
English translation.

Attempting polyphonic motets. It is not easy to begin teaching a polyphonic motet to a choir that is not yet experienced enough to sight-
read all the voice-parts at once. Playing it to them on the piano will
not give them a very clear impression of the music, because the better
the counterpoint, the more difficult it is to make it sound convincing
on a keyboard. In 'Deo gratias' it would be more helpful to start with
the single threads of sound on which the motet is founded. Begin with
the sopranos singing their strong opening phrase. (The 'ti' of
'gratias' is pronounced 'tz'.) Then let the basses sing their version of
it in bars 2–3. Next, the altos' rising phrase in their first three bars,
followed by the tenors' entry in imitation. If the basses then sing bars
4–6, everyone will recognize that it links both phrases, and later on
they will be able to hear that these two phrases are the foundation
of the whole motet. When each part has been learnt separately to
the end, try combining the altos and basses, while the others follow
their own voice-part in silence. Then try combining the sopranos
and tenors, with the others listening and imagining the sound of
their own phrases. In counterpoint that is as skilfully written as
this, one can practise any two voice-parts together, and the combined sounds will make musical sense. It should then be possible to
attempt to sing it in four parts.

71

Ex. 45

William Byrd (1605)

Conducting the entries in polyphonic music. It is the entries after a rest that need most help from a conductor during a polyphonic motet. When you have memorized Ex. 45, practise the leads in solitude, and imagine the sound of each entry. The following suggestions for bringing in the voices are meant for a choir that is grouped with its sopranos, altos, tenors, and basses in the same positions as in Fig. VII. (See page 29.)

BAR	VOICE	CONDUCTOR'S HAND
1	altos	*right*
	tenors	*left*
2	basses	*right*
3	sopranos	*left*
4	basses	*right*
	tenors	*left*
5	sopranos	*left*
6	altos	*right*
7	basses	*right*
8	tenors	*left*
	sopranos	*left*
9	altos	*right* (This is not after a rest, but it is the main theme and needs a firm beginning)

Try this in front of a mirror, to see whether your gestures are calm and not too large. Both hands will be moving continuously from the beginning to the end of the motet, but the beats that are *not* bringing in the entries should be very small and smooth.

Aiming at a clear texture. Polyphonic music is so eventful that it needs a clear texture to make it intelligible. Subtle variety in the dynamics can be a help. When one of the voices has a repetition of the words without a rest between the phrases, the second phrase is usually meant to be sung more quietly. In Ex. 45 this applies to the altos in bar 3 and to the tenors in bar 6, but not to any voice in the last three bars, where the counterpoint is working up to the climax of the music.

PART VIII

Editions

21. Differences of opinion among editors of early music

Editing. Amateurs have to rely on the help of an editor if they want to sing music that was written before the middle of the eighteenth century. Professionals can occasionally perform early music from a facsimile of the first edition, but no beginners' choir could manage to read a motet such as Byrd's 'Deo gratias' (Ex. 45) from the original notation, because the signs and symbols would look too unfamiliar. An editor's first job is to decide what the composer meant: he then has to rewrite the music in modern notation.

Part-books. Sixteenth-century editions of madrigals and motets were printed in separate part-books, with a single line for each voice. It is not difficult to get used to singing choral music from a single melodic line, but most choirs are happier if they can see what the other voice-parts are supposed to be doing.

Clefs. In early editions the C clef was used on the middle line of the stave for the altos and on the next line up for the tenors. This custom, which lasted until the nineteenth century, was more satisfactory than our modern use of the clefs in choral music, as it avoided leger lines for the altos and it spared the tenors from having to transpose their part an octave lower. Unfortunately there seems little chance of a return to the C clef in choral writing.

Dynamics. There were no written indications for loud or soft in the original sixteenth-century part-books: any dynamics found in modern publications are editorial suggestions, as in Exs. 43–45. Seventeenth-century composers sometimes wrote 'loud' or 'soft' at moments of special contrast. (See Ex. 52, page 128.) The indications f and p

were used during the early eighteenth century, but performers were not given the frequent directions that we now depend on.

Accidentals. Our rules about accidentals date from the middle of the eighteenth century. Editors of earlier music often have to guess whether a written B should be sung B♭ or whether a written F should be sung F♯. Opinions differ, and one can find rival editions of the same piece of music where the semitones do not coincide.

Bar-lines. Sixteenth-century part-books were printed without bar-lines. This had its advantages, for the singers could see how to phrase by following the sense of the words and the shape of the tune. In Ex. 44, for instance, the altos would have found it much easier to sight-read the unexpected rhythm of the last two bars with a minim D instead of two crotchets tied over a bar-line. Choral conductors have to spend a good deal of their time trying to get rid of unwanted accents on a weak syllable at an editorial first beat. (See Ex. 45, where, on four occasions, the weak syllable 'o' of 'Deo' arrives at the first crotchet of a bar.)

Underlay of words. The words of the songs in sixteenth-century part-books were seldom written exactly underneath the notes that belonged to them. Editors must guess where each syllable should be.

Speeds. Madrigal composers never wrote 'quick' or 'slow' at the beginning of a piece of music: they left it to their singers to find out the speed of the song. Their written time-values were different from ours, and an editor has to change their minims into crotchets to suit our modern notation. There was a tradition that music written in breves and semibreves was meant to be performed very quickly, while music written in quavers was taken at a fairly slow speed. This tradition lasted until the early eighteenth century, and although Italian terms such as Allegro, Andante, and Adagio were in use by then, they had subtly different meanings from our modern definitions.

Time signatures. Editors of sixteenth-century music have to change the obsolete time-indications of circles and half-circles into our modern 'fractional' time signatures, which came into existence in the 1690s.

Ornaments and gracing. Ornaments were essential in all music written between 1650 and 1750. The composers trusted their performers to 'grace' the music, and modern editors have to suggest how this should be done. Trills at the cadences, which were the most frequently used ornaments, should not be attempted by inexperienced singers. But amateur choirs can be encouraged to grace the flowing rhythm of a tune such as Ex. 53 (page 129), where the dotted minim in the last bar sounds more expressive with a leaning appoggiatura. (For information about grace-notes, see page 151, under 'Suggestions for further reading'.)

Dotted notes and 'inequality'. Baroque composers often wrote quavers which look as if they were meant to be of equal length, but which were intended to be performed unevenly, either as a dotted quaver followed by a semiquaver, or as a semiquaver followed by a dotted quaver. There is an example in Ex. 48 (page 125) where Purcell's irony at the word 'dreadful' is subtly stressed by the inequality that the editors have suggested for the sopranos at the beginning of bar 4. The actual written dotted notes in baroque music had only an approximate length, which varied according to the mood of the piece. They could be as spiky and exaggerated as doubly dotted notes. Or they could relax into triplets, as in Ex. 62 (page 137) where Handel himself has suggested the skipping rhythm at the word 'holiday'.

Editors' realizations. The word 'realization', in its sense of 'brought into practical existence', is not only used in connection with an editor's realization of a figured bass: it also implies his decisions about the various problems of notation mentioned in this chapter.

Choosing which edition to use. When you are looking for music for your choir to sing you will possibly disagree with some of the things that an editor has done: he may have put $f\!f$ where you would have preferred pp, or Allegro when you would rather have had an Andante. Before buying any copies of early music it is as well to find out what other editions are available.

22. Available publications

Publishers' lists. Most music publishers are willing to send their classified lists of publications to anyone who asks for them.

Searching in music shops. If you live in or near a town or city where there is a good retail music shop you will be able to look through dozens of possibilities before buying a few single copies to take home and study at your leisure. Never hurry over your decision about what you would like your choir to sing. Where there are several editions of a work to choose from, do not be over-influenced by the difference in price. If the most expensive version is the best, it will be worth paying for, in order to avoid future frustration.

Borrowing from a library. It is now possible for conductors to borrow sets of choral music from public libraries. The length of time for which copies may be kept varies from place to place, but three months is quite usual. The county libraries are better at providing music than most of the municipal or borough libraries, but the librarian of my own county has assured me that 'this should not deter the would-be borrower from making contact with his local library; all public libraries in this country are linked in an inter-lending scheme which goes a long way towards making available to the individual a vast range of material'. If you are able to borrow music from a library you must insist that all members of the choir sign for their copies before taking them home after a practice. This may seem fussy, but it is the only way that your choir librarian can find out which member is guilty of losing a copy.

Hiring from a publisher. If you are unsuccessful in borrowing copies from a library, you may be able to hire them from the publisher. The charge for this is by the month. As with borrowed music, no marks must ever be made in ink or indelible pencil, and a list of names should be kept of those who take copies home.

Music that is out of print. A piece of music may be temporarily unobtainable because it is reprinting, or it may be irretrievably out-of-print because the publisher has decided that there is not enough demand for it to justify the expense of reprinting it. If you possess only one copy of an out-of-print work that you want your choir to sing, you may possibly feel tempted to run off a couple of dozen copies on an office duplicator. This is illegal.

The law of copyright. When a composer has a work accepted by a publisher, they both sign an agreement: the publisher promises to pay the composer a percentage of what he gets from the sale of each copy, and the composer promises that he will not let anyone else publish that piece of music. The law of copyright protects both of them from any unscrupulous people who try to possess copies without paying for them. Unfortunately there are music-lovers who are so ignorant about copyright that they never hesitate to make their own duplicated copies, even when the music is still in print. This means that they are stealing from the composer and the publisher, who both have to earn a living. Conductors should know the following facts:

The law of copyright protecting a composer also applies to an editor of early music and to a collector of traditional folk tunes.

A printed warning can be found as a footnote on the first page of many part-songs, saying: 'The copying of this work by hand in any form—on blackboard or on MS paper—is strictly forbidden as contrary to the Copyright Act of 1911.' This statement is no longer true. It was altered in the 1956 revision of the copyright law, when the international sign © came into use. Anyone may now make *a single copy* of any piece of music, without breaking the law. But it is still illegal to make more than one copy.

A work published during a composer's lifetime is not free of copyright until fifty years after his death. (If a work is published after the composer's death it is still copyright until fifty years after the date of publication.)

There are other clauses in the copyright law which are so complicated that they need an expert to disentangle them. But an amateur conductor can never go wrong if he always begins by asking the publisher's permission before making his own copies of a work.

Duplication. If you want your choir to sing an out-of-print part-song, the publisher may agree to duplicate some copies which he will hire to you by the month. Or he may allow you to get the copies duplicated yourself, though he will probably insist that they must be kept on his premises while they are not in use. It is worth having the copies made professionally through a duplicating agency: the dye-line process is cheap. Amateur duplicating is easy on office equipment such as a dry photocopier, and the result can be clear enough for reference copies. But the notes may not be dark enough for the singers to sight-read, and the thin paper will need to be backed if the pages are to survive the weekly choir practices. Duplicated copies should never be left in strong sunlight or near a fire.

23. Writing out music for the singers to use

Music-copying. There are many occasions when the conductor of an amateur choir has to write manuscript parts for his singers. The detailed advice in this chapter is for those who have not yet done any music-copying. The first thing to do is to get the necessary permission from the copyright owner. Then, before attempting to write out the music, try and have a few lessons from an experienced copyist who will show you how to save time by making the heads of the notes quite small and by joining them to the stems, whenever possible, with a single movement of the hand.

Finding a comfortable position. Sit at the right height. The table must be large enough for both your elbows to rest on it while you are writing. The light should come from a window or a lamp on your left. Some people find it a help to work with a sloping book-rest in front of them, as in a library.

Choice of manuscript paper. It is worth taking trouble to find the sort of manuscript paper that suits you best. A smooth surface can help the flowing movement of the pen, but professional copyists sometimes prefer a paper that offers a certain amount of resistance to the nib. Never use paper that has a porous texture. The page should be thick enough to prevent the writing from showing through on the other side. Avoid a greyish colour with faint staves. Cream-coloured paper does not reproduce as well as white on most duplicating machines. Before buying the paper, look at the left corner at the bottom of the page: if the manufacturer has printed his trade-mark immediately below the stave there will be no room to write any leger lines or words in the first bar of that line. And if the margins at the sides of the page are too narrow, there will be no room for writing such words as 'soprano' or 'alto'. Whenever possible, choose a manuscript paper that has more depth of space between the staves than the depth of the stave itself, as this will allow enough room for writing the words of the song. The size of the page should not be too large for the members of the choir to stand close together while holding out their copies.

Nibs. The ideal nib for music copying is wide enough to produce the head of a crotchet at a touch, and flexible enough to draw the thinnest of strokes. Professional copyists save time by using either a fountain pen or a 'reservoir' nib that holds more ink than a normal nib. Always clean your nib when you have finished writing.

Ink. Black ink is the easiest to read and it is the most satisfactory for any method of duplication. Avoid Indian ink, which is difficult to use. There are special black inks suitable for music-copying. (See page 153, under 'Equipment'.) Do not use the same bottle for longer than about three months, as it deteriorates with age. Shake the bottle before you begin work, and always close it when you stop writing.

Transparencies. Manuscripts can be duplicated by the dye-line method much more quickly and cheaply if the music is written on special sheets of single-sided transparent paper. Many professional copyists prefer transparencies to ordinary manuscript paper, because mistakes are easier to correct. If you have never done any music copying before, it would be as well to get used to writing on ordinary paper before attempting transparencies.

Avoiding smudges. When you have finished writing out a page of music, put it safely aside to dry. If you are compelled to use blotting paper in an emergency, choose a thick 'double-blotter' quality, and find a clean surface every time you need it, to avoid smudging the manuscript. It will help to protect the page of music if you put a sheet of ordinary typing paper under your hand while you are writing: a sweaty hand or wrist can make the manuscript paper too greasy.

Correcting mistakes. When you make a mistake, blot it immediately and scratch it out with a very sharp pen-knife. Before writing the correct note in its place, smooth the scratched-out surface with the flat blade of the pen-knife. Write the correct note with a soft lead pencil, and then ink it in very lightly, using no pressure on the nib. Leave it to dry. Corrections can be tiresome when the copy has to be duplicated: the sensitive process exaggerates any slight mark on the page, with the result that the scratched-out surface appears as a blur and the ghost of the wrong note remains as a permanent reproach. If you make several mistakes in the same bar, it is better to cover them up with a patch.

Planning the pages. Always number your page before you begin writing on it. If the copy is to be duplicated, remember that the photographic paper may be slightly smaller than your manuscript paper: anything you write in a margin must be as near as possible to the staves, to prevent it disappearing off the edge of the copy. Plan each page carefully, and begin on the left side of a double sheet of manuscript paper to avoid having to turn over unnecessarily. This is very important when the words of a second verse are placed as in Ex. 44. (Sometimes even publishers forget this obvious rule.)

Bar-lines. In choral scores the stave for each different voice—soprano, alto, tenor, or bass—has its own separate short bar-lines. When joining the staves at the beginning of each new line of the music it is as well to use a ruler. Professional copyists often prefer to have a special pen for ruling bar-lines. (Avoid cheap ball-point pens, as they can be uncontrollably messy.) While planning your page you may find it a help to put a faint pencil mark where you think the bar-lines should come. This will save you from getting stranded only half-way through a bar when you reach the end of a line.

Spacing. The time-pattern in every bar should be spaced so that sight-readers can recognize the rhythm of the music at a glance. Bad spacing in a manuscript copy or in a printed edition can be an annoying hindrance to professionals as well as to amateurs.

Writing the words under the music. Be careful to leave enough room for the words when you plan the spacing of the page. You should think of the written length of the syllables while you are writing the notes. And in polyphonic music you should be aware of the need to align the other voices. (See Fig. XIV, page 83, for an example of a well-

O LORD, MAKE THY SERVANT ELIZABETH OUR QUEEN TO REJOICE

William Byrd (edited I.H.)

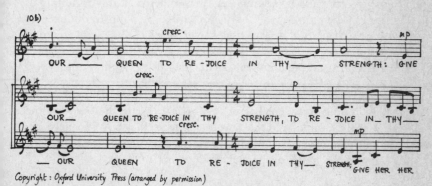

Fig. XIV

A sectional chorus score, omitting the parts for tenors and basses. The instrumental opening is shown as a cue.

spaced sectional chorus score.) Hyphens often have to be used when spacing words under their appropriate notes. (Advice about the correct division into syllables is mentioned on page 151.) You should resist the temptation to write the words rapidly in your normal handwriting, as this may not be clear enough for the singers to read. For a foreign text it may be better to write in small capitals, to avoid any doubts about the letters 'n', 'r', and 'u'.

Single voice-parts. Writing out single voice-parts is much easier than writing chorus scores, because there is no aligning. The singers, however, will need written cues before coming in after several bars rest, to give them confidence to pitch the notes of their next entry. If the music has modulated just before the entry, it is as well to show the whole chord of the new key. When there is no modulation, it is enough to give the last few notes and words of the nearest voice-part. Dynamics should also be shown in a cued-in part, so that the singers can judge how relatively loud or soft their next entry should be. You will probably need to use a different nib for cues, as the notes must be smaller than in the voice-parts. (See Fig. XIV.)

Numbering the bars. Choral works with orchestral accompaniment are marked with rehearsal figures or letters of the alphabet, for referring to any possible starting-place when a particular passage has to be practised. These are not essential in a short part-song: the conductor just says: 'Go back to page 2, line 4, bar 3.' Editors sometimes show the bar-numbers. This can be done by dividing the bars equally into 5, 10, 15, 20, etc. Or the bars can be numbered at the beginning of each new line. The second way is preferable in manuscript music: it is easier to read, and it saves time if everyone knows exactly where to look before counting. Single voice-parts without rehearsal figures will always need bar-numbers, as the lengths of the lines may vary.

Checking what you have written. Always check everything. It may seem to take a long time, but it will be worth it. Write the title and the name of the composer at the top of each page: the copy may get torn, and separate pages are not always easy to identify. At the foot of the page, add the name of the copyright owner.

Music-copying as an aid to memorizing. Always try to hear in your mind's ear the imagined sound of the notes you are copying, and, whenever possible, let your pen move in the rhythm of the music. This can be a great help in memorizing a work before conducting it.

24. Translations

Altering an editor's translation. There may be occasions when you will want to alter an editor's English translation of a choral work. Translating takes a good deal of time, and there is never enough room in the printed copy for writing the alternative words under their appropriate notes. But if you are dissatisfied with the editor's version it will be worth making an effort to save your choir from the vague platitudes of an inadequate translator.

Changing the order of the words. In translating a work such as a Bach cantata, one of the chief problems is the different word-order in the construction of German and English sentences. Bach always shaped his phrases according to the meaning of the words he was setting: the strength or the subtlety of each important noun or verb can be recognized in his harmonies. An English translator must never allow a dramatic chord to arrive on an unimportant word. This is one of the first things to look for if you are choosing between two editions of the same work.

Unsuitable vowels or consonants. A translator has to avoid reaching the height of a phrase on an uncomfortable vowel: a word such as 'peace' is difficult to sing quietly on a high note. The choice of consonants can also be a problem: an energetic attack on a word beginning with 'tr' will lose most of its strength if the consonant has to be changed to 'l' in the translation.

The need to avoid false accentuation. Translators of Bach often have difficulty with the '-en', which is the final syllable of so many of the German verbs that come at the end of a sentence. It is a sound that exactly suits the relaxed resolution of a cadence in a chorale. A translator who puts a strong single-syllabled English verb or noun in its place will be in danger of destroying Bach's phrasing if he disregards the tension and relaxation of the harmony.

Altering the exact translation for the sake of the phrasing. Most editions of the Bach *Passions* keep to the exact English words of any direct quotations from the bible. This can damage the music. For example, in the chorus from the *St. John Passion* quoted in Fig. XV (*a*) the clipped quavers and emphatic consonants are characteristic of the harsh determination of the High Priests and Pharisees. In Fig. XV (*b*) the English version from the authorized bible softens this mood with its mellow consonants and legato slurs. It would be better to alter the exact translation, as in Fig. XV (*c*), in order to keep the dramatic vitality of Bach's music.

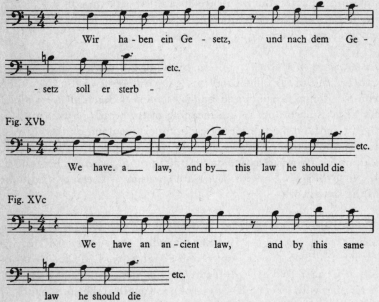

25. Piano reductions of orchestral accompaniments

Vocal scores. An editor of a work for chorus and orchestra has to provide a piano arrangement of the orchestral accompaniment for use during rehearsals. If you are going to venture on conducting an accompanied choral work you should look at any available editions and compare the piano parts to see which is the most suitable.

Reducing the essential sounds to the capacity of two hands on a keyboard. A piano arrangement must include everything that is essential for learning the work. This needs skill, owing to the limited stretch of a pianist's hands. A certain amount of compromise will be necessary. The correct spacing of a string orchestra's repeated *pp* chord of C will be impossible to reproduce on a keyboard if the violins are high up and the violas' E is a tenth above the cellos' C. Bringing the violas down an octave to suit the pianist's left hand will produce a stodgy sound that is utterly unlike what the composer intended. This is only one of the many problems that the writer of a vocal score has to try and solve.

The unplayable notes that have to be left out. If choir members are not given the opportunity to become familiar with what is going on in the accompaniment while they are still learning their own notes they will feel bewildered when they have to sing the work with an orchestra. Phrases that are unplayable on the keyboard should at least be hinted at in the printed copy. If the piccolo's high, rapid *ff* semiquavers are impossible for the pianist to combine with the low-lying crotchets of the main tune they should be indicated in small notes for several bars, followed by the word 'etc.', to warn the singers of the sort of thing they will be hearing.

Manipulating the unpianistic sounds. There are many orchestral sounds which are difficult to imitate on the piano. A vocal score should suggest the nearest equivalent. For instance, when slow held chords on woodwind and brass have a gradual crescendo from *pp* to *ff*, the piano reduction should if possible show a tremolando in brackets, to support the singers while they are building up their climax.

Details of instrumentation. The best piano reductions give frequent indications of the original instrumentation, with abbreviations such as Fl., Tpt., Timp., or Vla. written above or below the stave at appropriate moments in the vocal score. It is a great help to the pianist to see staccato notes marked 'Str. (pizz.)' or an *sfp* marked 'Brass (muted)'. And this gives the members of the choir a clearer idea of what to expect when they first sing with an orchestra.

PART IX

Accompaniment

---

26. Conducting with a stick

The stick as an extension of the hand. Before you attempt to conduct an accompanied choral work you will need to learn to use a stick. This will make it easier for the players to see your beat. It can also make it easier for you to avoid wasting too much energy while you are trying to control the rhythm. The stick should feel like a natural extension of your own hand and arm.

Choosing a stick. It is worth taking trouble to find the right stick that will suit you. (See page 153, under 'Equipment'.) You can choose between one with its varnished surface painted white, or one that has the natural colour of the wood. White sticks are easier to see, especially by artificial light. The point of the stick should be as narrow as a blunt pencil. The other end can either be shaped so that it widens into a small wooden bulb, or it can be fitted into a cork handle. Cork has the advantage of absorbing some of the sweat from a conductor's hand. You can shorten your stick to the right length: fourteen or fifteen inches will be quite long enough. Avoid choosing a stick that is too heavy: you should never have to use it by grasping the handle as if it were a bread-knife. A stick has to be perfectly balanced if it is to feel like an extension of your arm. Hold it easily and waggle it swiftly to and fro or up and down: if the balance is correct, it will quiver as if it had a life of its own.

Holding the stick. Take the cork handle between your forefinger and thumb. Find the most comfortable place: neither too near the end of the stick nor too far down towards the point. Then let your middle finger just touch your forefinger, lightly supporting the feather-weight balance of the stick. (Plate c.) If you grip too tightly, the stick will remain rigid: relax until it feels sensitive enough to respond to any movement. You will probably drop it several times, but it will be unlikely to break if it just falls gently to the floor. (You will need to have several spare sticks, however, as there will be other occasions on which they may get broken.)

Exercises for getting used to the feel of a stick. Walk round the room with the stick in your hand and lightly flick an imaginary speck of dust from at least twenty different places on the walls and the furniture. Stand in the middle of the room and trace in mid-air the outline of the perspective of each door and window, using the point of your stick as if it were the tip of an artist's paint-brush: do this in a leisurely fashion at first, and then repeat it as swiftly as you can. Write your signature in imaginary letters on the ceiling. Move your arm very slowly in a wide semicircle from left to right, while counting up to sixteen: at each new number, give a slight indication with the tip of your stick, as if you were counting the singers in the front row of your choir. Try the circling exercises suggested in Chapter 9, paragraphs 5, 6, and 7 (for the right arm only, without any support): feel that the tip of the stick is a true extension of your hand. (See Plate d.)

Applying a hand technique to the use of a stick. The 'clock-face' exercise suggested on page 30 is useful when learning to apply a hand technique to the use of a stick. Try it in front of a mirror, and be sure that your stick is not pointing away from the direction of your beat. (You should not allow yourself to be influenced by press photographs showing a celebrated conductor with his stick pointing down the back of his neck. Photographers seldom give us a picture of the concentrated placing of a beat: they prefer to capture the more dramatic moments at a rehearsal.) A stick can never disguise an inadequate technique: in fact, it will seem to exaggerate any awkward jerks or flabby meanderings. But if you have already achieved a reliable technique in conducting with your hand, the stick will never be a hindrance. It can help you to control the rhythm of any accompanied choral music, whether it is with piano, organ, or orchestra.

27. Amateur pianists

Finding the right pianist. Good amateur accompanists are rare. If you are fortunate enough to find a sensitive, reliable pianist who is willing to play for your practices you will be spared having to face one of the most difficult problems in choir-training. Conductors are often obliged to play their own accompaniments, dodging up and down; hovering between sitting and standing; filling in the piano part with one hand while conducting the vocal entries with the other. This is the method used by repetiteurs in an opera house, and it can prove invaluable in the education of a professional conductor, but it is not necessarily the best way for an amateur to learn choral conducting. If you cannot find an experienced accompanist, you should choose someone who is capable of learning what is wanted.

The practical experience needed in accompanying a choir. A choral accompanist has to be prepared to play much more than the printed piano part. Each vocal line may be asked for in turn, over the instrumental bass part. When the time comes to combine all the voices, the pianist should be able to reduce the four vocal lines to their essential harmonies, while providing as much as possible of the written piano part. A good accompanist always knows what each voice is supposed to be doing, and can instantly supply the right notes whenever they are needed.

Some faults of inadequate pianists. The piano is a difficult instrument. Few things are more frustrating than being compelled to work with an accompanist who is incapable of playing *legato*, and who is either too loud or too soft. Inadequate pianists hurry when the music is technically difficult, and drag when they are faced with stretchy chords or with a lot of quick notes, or when there are leaps of over an octave, or—what is perhaps their worst difficulty—when the contrapuntal vocal parts have to be divided between the two hands.

The habit of over-pedalling. Inexperienced pianists very often indulge in over-pedalling. The feel of the foot on the pedal gives them a false confidence. It is no good saying: 'Don't use so much pedal': your pianist will not be able to give up this bad habit without some drastic cure such as having to sit with the right foot curled round the nearest leg of the chair.

'*Putting in the expression*.' Unwanted rubato is a fault which many pianists are guilty of. One of their worst crimes is the sentimental slowing-down just before the entry of the voices. This deflates the singers, who are poised for their first note, and it is infuriating for the conductor. If this happens to you, it will be no use shouting 'ONE, TWO, THREE' from a distance: you will have to go and stand near the pianist and exert all your strength of purpose to rescue the rhythm.

The position of the piano during a choir practice. The right position for the piano will be one that enables the player to see the beat while looking at the music. An upright piano is often placed with its back against a wall: if it is too heavy to move, the conductor will have to go and stand next to it all the time.

Moving a piano. If you want to move an upright piano into a more suitable position you must take care not to jerk it too much: in an elderly instrument the action may tilt so that the strings are no longer in contact with the dampers, and it will then sound as if the pedal was permanently held down. Moving a grand piano is easier, but this also needs care. Look at the angle of the castors before you begin: then move it very slowly, so that it cannot glide away from you. Never ask volunteer helpers to move a piano without having one person in charge, to tell the others exactly where it is to go, and to give the word when to start moving. A grand piano needs at least three people to move it. Pushing is better than pulling.

Keeping a piano in good condition. Pianos need regular use. And they should be regularly tuned: if possible, every three months. A piano, like a human being, must be neither too cold nor too hot. It must have air, and it should not be muffled day and night under a heavy covering. But avoid draughts. And, above all, avoid damp, which is the worst enemy. Clean the keys with spirit, not with water. Dust it frequently, but never use a feather dusting brush when the lid is open. It is unwise to leave vases of flowers on the top of a piano: if they are knocked over, the water may leak into the action. This warning also applies to bottles, and to glasses for drinks. Metal objects such as ash-trays and photograph frames should not be put on the top of a piano as they can set up a jarring sound.

28. Amateur organists

Good and bad organists. A good organist can help a choir by supporting the sustained harmonies, by 'breathing with the singers' and phrasing so as to let in the air between sentences, by varying the texture so that each contrapuntal entry can be clearly distinguished, and by colouring the words to bring out each dramatic change in the music. Good organists, however, are as rare as good pianists, and you may have to do the best you can with an inexperienced player. But avoid, if possible, the sort of bad organist who thinks of himself as a soloist, and who grudges having to accompany your amateur singers.

The organist with a lust for power. A bad organist can do much more damage than a bad pianist. The instrument, with its built-in amplification, can get louder and louder without any effort on the part of the player. This is a dangerous temptation to those who like to feel that they are powerful.

The distressing compromise of having to 'follow' an organist. The post of church organist is not always the best preparation for learning to follow a conductor's beat. Many organists are so used to having their own way on Sundays that they take it for granted they will always be responsible for starting or stopping, and for asserting each change of speed. If you are unlucky enough to be lent one of these dictatorial players to accompany your choir in a choral work, you may find yourself abandoning all hope and following what the organist chooses to do. This can be torture. It will, however, be a useful lesson in adapting your beat to what is beyond your control. It will teach you how to scramble from one beat to the next without getting frantic, and how to prolong a beat indefinitely without dithering. It will also teach you the necessity for showing a clear down beat, whatever else may be happening.

The organist's difficulty in seeing the beat. Church organs are often placed at one side of the chancel. This makes it difficult for the organist to watch the beat. He has to rely on having a small adjustable mirror in which he can catch sight of the conductor's reflection out of the corner of his eye. If your organist is worried by this, you may find it safer to have a sub-conductor standing beside him and imitating all your gestures. It is as well to practise this before a rehearsal.

The conductor's difficulty in hearing the organ. It is almost impossible for a choral conductor to hear the actual sound of an organ accompaniment while the choir is singing. If it is loud enough for him to hear all the instrumental details through the voices, it will probably be much too loud for the balance of the music. In most churches the sound of the organ travels up to the roof and spreads through the building: there will almost certainly be a slight time-lag in certain parts of the church, and from where he is standing the conductor may not hear the notes until after they have been played. This is difficult to get used to. You will find that you have to have faith in the feel of the rhythm and in the imagined sound in your inner ear. Ask someone to listen to the balance and the synchronization from the far end of the church. And be sure that your singers have learnt the music so thoroughly that they will be able to follow the look of your beat without waiting to hear the sound of the organ.

29. Amateur orchestras

Choral singing with orchestral accompaniment. Conducting an amateur orchestra is a subject that needs a whole book to itself. The practical advice offered in this chapter is intended for the choral conductor who has a chance of borrowing an existing amateur orchestra for a few combined rehearsals with his own choir.

Score-reading. It is possible to learn a good deal about score-reading in solitude. There are books on orchestration which give details of each instrument, mentioning its compass, the method of technique for producing the notes, and the individual characteristics of the tone-colour. (See page 151.) Small study scores are published, which can be followed during broadcasts, or while listening to a record. Score-reading, however, is only of practical use to a conductor if it is combined with the experience of playing an orchestral instrument.

Inevitable shortcomings of a beginners' orchestra. No choir-trainer should attempt to conduct an amateur orchestra until he knows what it feels like to play in one. If you join a beginners' orchestra, your first practice is likely to be a test of endurance. The tuning-up will prove an alarming ordeal for some of the players: cellists' pegs will slip; an inexperienced oboist, when asked to establish the A, will produce an agitated A♯; a clarinet player, while struggling with the difficulties of the 'break', will let out a high squawk; and an anxious flautist, though vehemently puffing, will remain quite inaudible. If you yourself are playing an instrument that you have only recently begun learning, you will be able to sympathize with your fellow-members of the orchestra. And you will find out what it is like to be at the mercy of an amateur conductor. When he suddenly says: 'Start at letter K,' you will realize that it takes quite a long time to get your instrument into position and to get the right note to come in on. When there is a pause over a note, you will learn that you need a good deal of courage to take your eyes off the copy in order to watch the beat. And you will discover how uncomfortable it can be to have to share a music stand with another player who may want it at a different height and angle from your own line of vision. If you are playing percussion you will know what it feels like to count 57 bars rest and then come in on an *ff* cymbal clash without any encouraging sign from your conductor, who may be entirely occupied with a difficult entry for the brass. Or, after counting 56 bars, you may hear the conductor stopping everyone in order to criticize the strings, just as you were about to play your one note in the whole movement. All this practical experience, however painful it may be, will prove useful when you conduct your first choral rehearsal accompanied by an amateur orchestra.

Marking the orchestral parts. One of the most important things in preparing for a combined rehearsal is the thorough checking of the orchestral material. If the parts are hired you will have to rub out the previous players' marks before writing in your own. Elementary string players need the signs ⊓ and ∨ to show whether they are to play down-bow or up-bow. (See Fig. XVI.)

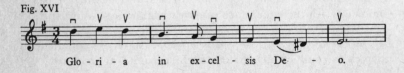

Fig. XVI

Glo - ri - a   in   ex - cel - sis   De   -   o.

These bowing marks may look fussy, but the cross-rhythm, which the singers can recognize from the words, will not be obvious to the players unless they are given some help. Bowing marks will tell them about the phrasing. And with the right phrasing the music will make sense, in spite of any roughness in the orchestral sound. When checking the parts, you must be sure that all the other phrase marks, such as slurs and dynamics, are correctly shown: a previous conductor's pencilled instructions about a rallentando can wreck your players' attempts to follow what you are trying to convey to them. And check the rehearsal figures, to see that the orchestral parts agree with the chorus scores.

The seating plan. Before conducting your first rehearsal with an orchestra you should write a plan of the position of every instrumentalist in the strings, woodwind, brass, and percussion sections, so that you will know where each player will be sitting. (See Fig. XVII for a suggested seating plan.) Memorize this plan, and practise conducting your score in solitary silence, bringing in each instrumental entry. You will need to use your left hand for some of these entries, as in the contrapuntal leads for 'Deo Gratias' mentioned on page 74.

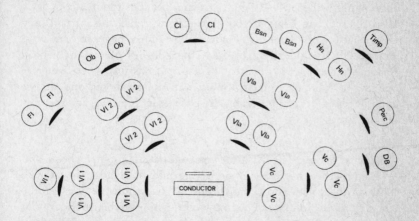

Fig. XVII

A seating plan which allows plenty of room for the amateur string players to spread themselves and for the conductor to walk between the desks at rehearsals.

Some idiosyncrasies in choral conducting which can prove disastrous with an orchestra. The basic technique of choral conducting can be applied to instrumental conducting, but choir-trainers sometimes get into habits which could prove disastrous when working with an orchestra.

(1) Facial expressions, which can be a help in unaccompanied singing, are no use to players who are too busy reading their notes to look at anything except the tip of the conductor's stick.

(2) The habit of raising the beat high in the air for a sudden pianissimo upsets the nearest string players, who are unable to alter the working level of their line of vision.

(3) The habit of not indicating silent first beats during piano rehearsals can lead to chaos with an orchestra. The pianist, with the complete printed vocal score in front of him, will have been able to keep going while the conductor moulds the shape of each phrase between his fingers as if it were an unaccompanied madrigal. But the orchestral players cannot hope to know when to come in with their next phrase, especially if it follows several bars rest.

Turning the pages of a full score. The admirable habit of conducting unaccompanied choral music by heart without a score is not always advisable in works with orchestra. Learn the music by heart just as thoroughly as if you were going to conduct it without a copy, but keep the score in front of you at orchestral rehearsals: it will save time when things go wrong. There will be a lot of pages to turn over. Practise this while going through the gestures of conducting an imaginary choir and orchestra. If a page ends just where you are needing both hands for contrapuntal entries, you should find a more suitable place for turning. Mark these places in the score, and memorize the turns.

Problems of balance. The first time you conduct a combined choral and orchestral rehearsal you will find it very difficult to judge the balance between the voices and the instruments. The choir may seem to be singing *pp* instead of *mf*. The first violins will probably sound louder than anyone else because they will be just under your ear. Never ask the first desk of violins to 'play softer' unless a trustworthy listener at the far end of the hall has told you that they are too loud. Orchestral conductors have to get used to not hearing a perfect balance from where they are standing. Brass and percussion can sound twice as loud to the people in the back row of the audience. And even professional conductors sometimes complain that a harpsichord is too loud when it is barely audible to most of the listeners.

Controlling the singers and players at a distance. Your choir will seem a long way away from you when it is placed behind an orchestra, even if everyone is sitting as close together as possible. In your efforts to control the rhythm you must not saw the air wildly with signals of despair. Resist the temptation to sing or shout or stamp. Do not lean forwards in a vain attempt to get closer to your singers and players: it will cripple your arm movements and will cause acute discomfort to the nearest viola players, who will try to dodge out of your way to avoid being hit. Let your gestures remain as precise as possible. A rhythmical beat can make itself felt on a large platform just as clearly as in a small room. Keep to the essentials of the technique you have been practising, and be aware of everyone else's difficulties while trying to forget your own. Confidence will come with experience, if you are thoroughly at home in the music that you have chosen to conduct.

PART X

Giving a concert

---

30. Organizing the event

The decision to perform in public. Sooner or later the members of your choir will say that they want to give a concert. Should they be allowed to? Amateur music-making that flourishes behind closed doors often wilts in front of an audience. But if your singers have already given pleasure to anyone who has happened to hear them, and if they are demanding 'something to work at', you might as well let them find out what it feels like to sing in public.

Delegating the work. Even an informal charity concert needs careful planning. You may think it would be easier to decide on everything yourself; to carry all the plans in your own head, and to be in direct contact with everyone concerned. But organizing a concert is not a one-man job. You will have to rely on the help of other people. And you will need to know how they are getting on with the various jobs you have given them.

Forming a committee. The easiest way to keep an eye on your helpers is to appoint a committee from among your choir members. Do not be put off by the formalities: the time-honoured words that are still in use are technical terms describing practical necessities. (If you know all about committees, leave out this paragraph and turn to the end of page 99.) *The Chairman,* who is by far the most important person on the committee, should be intelligent and generous: able to keep to the point during discussions and to prevent any jealous ill-feelings from getting in the way. All questions are addressed to the Chair. *The Secretary* should be able to take notes during meetings, and should ungrudgingly spend time and energy on keeping in touch with every member of the committee. A knowledge of shorthand is not necessary, and the typing can be done by an assistant. *The Treasurer* should be experienced in book-keeping. He should be responsible for seeing that a budget has been worked out, and he should make sure that details of comparative costs have been discussed before any money is spent. *The Agenda* is the list of subjects to be discussed. It is sent to each member of the committee several days before the meeting. *The Minutes* are the decisions that have been reached at the previous meeting: each headed paragraph is numbered in an order that is appropriate for discussion. It is the Secretary's job to 'take the Minutes', which means writing reports of the various conversations held during a meeting and then reducing them to the bare essentials, weeding out any pompous padding. The type-written Minutes are sent to each committee member. They are read out at the beginning of the meeting, and the Chairman asks if they may be 'approved'. This gives anyone a chance to question the accuracy of a paragraph, or to complain if anything important has been left out. When the Minutes have been approved, the Chairman signs them as correct. The signing of the Minutes is the first item on an Agenda. *'Arising from the Minutes'* is the second item on the Agenda. This gives members a chance to find out if the practical suggestions made at the last meeting have been put forward and acted on, or if they have been buried in the files and forgotten. *Subcommittees* can be formed if there are any special problems to be discussed, such as refreshments, transport, hospitality, etc. *Reports* from a subcommittee can be read aloud at committee meetings. The Treasurer can also read out his reports, but it is as well to have his remarks in writing, so that members who are slow at figures can take their time working them out. *'Any other business'* is the final heading on the Agenda: it can include suggestions that are not related to anything that has been discussed. The last item of 'Any other business' is fixing the date for the next meeting. (Do not feel exasperated at the thought of yet another meeting: a well-run committee can save you from the stress of worrying about what may not yet have been thought of, during the days just before the concert.)

General discussions. Your committee will be representing the whole choir, but you must have a general meeting for all the singers, so that they can say what kind of concert they want, and where and when it should be, and which charity it should be in aid of.

Finding a suitable date. You will need to fix your date several months in advance. If it is to be a summer concert, you may find that every Saturday afternoon from mid-May till the end of August is already booked for some local event. If it is to be a Christmas concert, there may be no free evening left during the last fortnight of December. Find out what dates have been fixed in all the nearby schools, colleges, churches, chapels, dramatic societies, and film clubs. Go to the Council Offices and ask to see the list of future events in the halls owned by the Council.

Choosing a suitable place. It is not easy to find the right place for an amateur concert. The following warnings are the result of many years' experience of being grateful for whatever is available. *Open-air concerts* are seldom as idyllic as they are meant to be. The peaceful atmosphere can be shattered by the noise of planes, lorries, or transistors. A high wind can suddenly spring up, with the result that the singers will appear to be mouthing their words in dumb show. To guard against this, you should place the choir in front of a wall or a high bank, with the prevailing wind behind them. Try not to be persuaded to install microphones. Mechanical amplification has a cruel way of exaggerating the weaknesses of an inexperienced choir. It also has a disintegrating effect on an audience: people begin strolling about and talking to each other after the first few minutes. Among many other problems, you will have to face the difficulty of providing seats for the audience: chairs are expensive to hire, and they are apt to sink into the soft earth and ruin a well-kept lawn. Remember that the listeners should not be compelled to sit with the glare of the sun in their eyes: you must notice the position of the trees when you are choosing the site, so that the audience as well as the singers can be in the shade. Midges and mosquitoes can disrupt a performance: you must warn your singers to bring the most effective insect-repellent they can find. A sudden downpour of rain can be catastrophic. Never plan an open-air event without making alternative arrangements for wet weather. Ask the Meteorological Office for the local forecast on the morning of the concert, and rely on their opinion rather than on your own. *A large house* can make an attractive temporary concert hall. But unless the owners are close friends, you will probably feel that you are getting in their way. There will be a house-party for the weekend; the domestic staff will have to find time to move the ancestral furniture from one room to another; and your singers, being unaccustomed to the slipperiness of the highly polished floor, will hesitate self-consciously as they sidle past the Waterford glass and the Sèvres china. *A school hall* is an obvious choice for amateur music-making. The old-fashioned sort can be very cold in winter, and you may find yourself conducting in a large room containing two small paraffin stoves, with a frozen audience sitting immovable in numb acquiescence, while your singers, at their very first note, disappear behind a cloud of their own breath. Such experiences, however, are rare in the nineteen-seventies. Most modern school halls are far too hot to conduct in at any time of the year: I have known dressing-rooms behind the stage where the conductor was expected to wait in a temperature of 83° F. between the items of a performance. Acoustics can be tricky in some modern buildings, and there may be the drawback of noisy air-conditioning mentioned on page 46. *Churches* can be dark as well as cold. But if you choose your church carefully, making sure of the warmth and the light as well as of the friendliness of the vicar, you will find a great deal to be thankful for. The seating will already be provided: the sidesmen, having shown the audience into their places, will take the collection for charity at the end of the performance, and will count it for you in the vestry. The vicar, if asked, will have mentioned the concert in his announcements on the previous Sunday. And there will probably be a car-park fairly near the entrance.

Financial arrangements. As soon as you have found the right place for your concert, you or the Treasurer of your committee must get the financial arrangements clearly set out in writing. You must know in advance how much you will be expected to contribute towards such expenses as heating, lighting, and cleaning. Nothing is more appalling at the end of a performance than to hear the voice of the vicar saying from his pulpit: 'The whole of the collection will be in aid of the church,' when you had previously arranged that he was to take only fifty per cent. (This may sound an unlikely occurrence, but it happened to me in a large church in the west of England in 1940, when I was working for what is now the Arts Council. It taught me that the choice of vicar matters more than anything else in organizing a church concert.) Any decisions taken at an interview or over the telephone must be put in writing at the first possible moment.

Send a letter, stating each point very clearly, and asking for a written confirmation of the facts. Keep a copy of the correspondence, and do not destroy it until the concert is over and all the bills are paid.

Publicity. You should not listen to any member of your committee who says: 'Don't let's bother about publicity: after all, people are sure to come to anything in aid of charity.' Nothing could be further from the truth. Friends and relations of your singers, moved by loyalty or curiosity, may fill three or four rows of pews in a fair-sized church. It will take a lot of hard work to fill another twenty rows. You will have to have leaflets printed. Five by eight inches is a useful small size for displaying in shop windows. (Someone will have to go from door to door, asking each owner's permission.) This size is also suitable for sending by post. Try and get local organizations to enclose your leaflets with any notices they are sending out, and ask your choir members to put one with each of the personal letters they are writing. Choose a suitable colour: black lettering on blue seldom shows up at a distance, and white on brilliant pink can look too dazzling. Use as few words as possible, but be sure to mention the date (including the year), the time, the place, the details of admission, and the name of the charity it is in aid of. Names of the conductor and any soloists are best left unadorned, without any mention of 'Mr.', 'Dr.', or 'A.R.C.O.'. Avoid the word 'artiste'. The plain word 'organ' is better than 'at the organ'. When you send your typewritten draft of the leaflet to the printer you should indicate the approximate spacing you want, as well as enclosing a specimen of the kind of lettering you would like him to use. Insist on seeing a proof, and take your time over correcting it carefully: proof-reading is not a job that should be entrusted to a subcommittee. The cost of printing leaflets will be expensive for the first few hundred. After that, the price will not increase as much as might be expected: it is therefore worth your while to order a fairly large number.

Advertising in the press. A mere couple of lines of advertisement in a local paper is usually a waste of money, but it can have surprisingly effective results if you persuade the editor to refer to the announcement of your concert in one of his gossip columns, linking it to some item of news in the neighbourhood.

The Performing Right Society. Many people who organize concerts are unaware of the existence of the Performing Right Society. Others, who have heard the name mentioned, are unwilling to learn what it involves, saying: 'Well, so far I've managed to get by without doing anything about the P.R.S.' This is against the law. Composers depend on their fees from the Performing Right Society to enable them to earn enough to live on. Although they get royalties from the sale of their published works under the Copyright Act mentioned on page 79, these sums are only a small proportion of what they need for an income: most of what they earn comes from fees for live performances, broadcasts, and recordings of the music they have written. The Performing Right Society collects these fees and distributes them. Anyone who gives a concert in public must send details of what is on the programme, so that the composers, editors, authors, and publishers may get their fair share of what they have earned. Do not make the mistake of thinking that your choir is too small and insignificant for the Performing Right Society to be concerned with what you are doing: the rules apply to amateurs as well as to professionals. The following extracts are taken from the notes which the secretary of the Music Classification Committee of the Performing Right Society sends to choral societies in answer to their questions:

Permission is necessary for any public performance [of copyright music] given outside the domestic circle of a particular individual, whether or not a charge is made for admission, [and] whether the concert takes place in a public hall or room or in a church. Music is often publicly performed for charitable purposes, but it is only in very special circumstances that we can justify the waiving of our members' royalties [i.e. performing fees] on such occasions.

The Society issues licences to proprietors of premises at which music is performed: you will normally find that municipally-owned buildings, schools owned by education authorities, as well as most Methodist churches and many church halls of all denominations are licensed by us. The cost of [these licences] is often passed on to hirers of premises by the addition of a small percentage to the hire fee.

Where your performance is covered by one of our licences we would ask only for your co-operation in completing the programme returns [i.e. forms.]

The details we need are:

- (*a*) Date of concert
- (*b*) Name and address of the premises
- (*c*) Titles and composers of works performed (and in the case of older works any editors, arrangers, translators and publishers)
- (*d*) The means of accompaniment: piano, organ, small or full orchestra.

When organizing your concert, find out if the building is licensed. If it is, ask for a form. If it is not, write to the Performing Right Society (address on page 156) for advice, and ask for a form to be sent to you. It would be as well to ask for several forms, as there is so little room for filling in the details that you will probably spoil a couple in your attempts to write small enough.

31. Planning the programme

Length of programme. Nearly all concerts of amateur music last much too long. If you are planning a programme of Christmas music in a church it should not go on for more than an hour. You must time the length of each item beforehand, allowing about fifty minutes for the actual music, and the remaining ten minutes for moving on and off the platform and for standing up or sitting down between items. There will be no need for an interval in a performance of this length.

The need for contrast. For your first attempt at giving a concert, an hour of unaccompanied choral music would be too great a strain, not only on the singers but also on the listeners. It would be better to join with any instrumental groups that you had already heard and had approved of. (*Never* ask anyone to perform at a concert for which you are responsible without knowing what sort of sounds they make and what sort of music they would be likely to choose.) Short items for strings or recorders can make a welcome contrast to unaccompanied singing. You would need to have at least two combined pieces, one at the beginning and one at the end, so that all the singers and players could join together.

Choosing the music. When you are discussing with the choir what the programme should be, you must be clear in your own mind about what you want to perform, and you must be able to convince your singers that it is just what they also are wanting to work at. If one of your sopranos says: '*Must* we do the Praetorius? Can't we have "Silent Night" instead?' you should remember that it is your job as an amateur conductor to work at the music that you are passionately keen on.

Planning the order of the programme. There will be practical reasons for the order in which you put some of the items. If the strings are to play alone, it would be as well to have them immediately after the first combined piece, before their instruments have had time to get out of tune. Aim at as much variety of texture as possible; for instance, the unaccompanied tenors and basses could be followed by a piece for descant and treble recorders. Avoid having two tunes that are slow and sad with nothing contrasting between them. Time signatures should be varied: it is a mistake to put two $\frac{6}{8}$ pieces one after the other. A satisfactory following-on of key signatures is very important in a programme of short items. If you have a group of three pieces, all in major keys, you should be careful not to have the second in the key that is a tone lower than the first, with a return to the original key for the third item: this has a deadening effect on the music. You should aim at planning a programme so that it has a convincing shape of its own. This is not easy to achieve, but it is worth all the time and thought that can be given to it.

32. Rehearsals

Preliminary rehearsals. It is unlikely that you will manage to get a full combined rehearsal before the day of the performance. Your preliminary rehearsals will have to be very thorough and you must be firm about absentees: if twelve rehearsals have been planned for the concert, you should not allow any member of the choir to miss more than four of them.

Teaching the choir to sing to an audience. Some of the members of your choir may think that they have to sing louder when there is an audience. Show them that it is possible to sing *pianissimo* so clearly that the sound will carry to a considerable distance. Let them imagine that they are singing to the people in the back row of a large audience, and remind them that the best way to project their voices is to pronounce their words with conviction.

Advice about 'stage-managing' a concert. The last choir practice before the combined rehearsal should be treated as if it were the dress rehearsal of a play. There will be no need for them to dress up for it, but you should find out what they intend to wear and use your tact to avoid any individual ostentation. (In planning what to wear yourself, remember that a conductor's back-view is what matters; also that you will need to feel free when raising your arms.) The position of each singer must be worked out in detail. Arrange the chairs in an order corresponding to the seating arrangements for the performance. (See Fig. XVIII, page 107, for a suggested seating plan in a church, allowing an uninterrupted line of vision between the organist and the conductor.)

You must ask the singers to practise standing up and sitting down between items as quietly as possible. (Try this out yourself, so that you can show them how it is done: keep your feet close together and *don't move them*; get up and sit down without bending forward from the waist; feel that the weight of your body is supported by the muscles of your calves and thighs.) When the singers are standing ready to begin, it is as well to ask them whether anyone in the front row intends to wear higher heels or a taller hair-style at the performance, as this could defeat your careful preparations for enabling everyone to see the beat. Implore the sopranos and altos not to get cluttered up with their handbags. Give each singer a typewritten programme: let them mark the items in which they are singing, and ask them to arrange their copies of the music in the right order. This will give you a chance to find out whether everyone has a copy of everything. You will also be able to make sure that each singer has written a pencilled reminder about how to get the first note of every unaccompanied song, so that no one will be in any doubt as to whether to listen for a pizzicato chord from the leading first violin or for a sustained key-note from the leading treble recorder. Remind them that while they are standing to sing they must hold all the copies of music that they will need throughout a whole group of songs: it looks

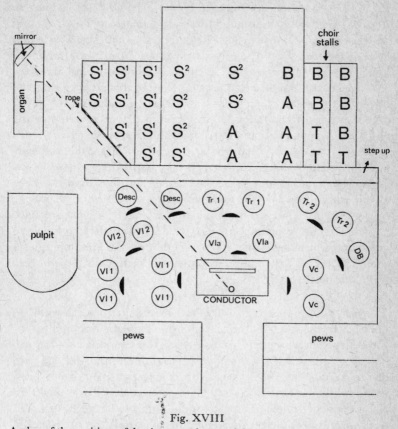

Fig. XVIII

A plan of the positions of the singers, strings, and descant and treble recorders for a church concert allowing an uninterrupted line of vision between organist and conductor.

very bad if individuals turn round and dump their unwanted items on their chairs.

Preparations for the combined rehearsal. Nothing should be left to chance. You will need to have discussed all your plans for a church concert with the vicar. He must approve of your choice of music. (I have met vicars who have refused to allow a medieval Latin carol in honour of the Virgin Mary to be sung in church.) The vicar must also have approved of the practical arrangements for the concert, including the tuning of the organ, the lighting of the chancel and nave, the hiring and transport of chairs for the singers and players, the use of the vestry for leaving coats and instruments, the use of the church hall's lavatories during the final rehearsal, the use of the church car-park for listeners and performers, and the borrowing of hymn-books for the audience to join in the last carol. You must find out if he would like to welcome the audience or to say a prayer before the concert begins, and you must ask him whether he wants to have applause or not. Applause can help to reduce the scared tension at an amateur performance, but it can also destroy the atmosphere of a carol concert with its loud and frequent interruptions. It is best to leave this decision to the vicar.

Things that can go wrong on the day. You should arrive at least half an hour before the combined rehearsal is due to begin, bringing two or three helpers with you. (This may seem over-cautious, but you can never know what will go wrong at the last minute, and on more than one occasion I have been faced with having to move a heavy brass lectern without any assistance.) The unexpected set-backs could include any of the following: the key of the organ will have disappeared (it is wise to take a screw-driver to the rehearsal); a coach-load of sightseers from the next county will arrive to look at the chancel tombs just as you were hoping to get the music stands in position; members of the Guild of Church Workers will come armed with huge vases of evergreens which they will place in front of the pulpit just where you had intended the second violins to sit; a road-drill will begin digging up the pavement outside the church porch, or a traffic diversion will cut off the access to the church car-park. (Either of these crises will teach you how important it is to consult the Council Office and the Police during the week before the performance.) The lorry bringing the hired chairs will not have appeared on time, and you will have to part with one of your assistants, so that he can find out what has happened. When the chairs arrive, you should see that there are strong, intelligent helpers to unload them and put them in position: give them copies of your seating plan, so that they know exactly what to do. (It is only incompetent organizers who insist on arranging chairs and carrying platforms while other people stand by and watch them: your job is to keep still so that you can answer the dozens of questions that everyone will want to ask you.) There will be chaos during the five minutes before the rehearsal. The organist's A will be greeted with groans of protest from the orchestra. (The organ should have been tuned very recently, as close to the day of the performance as possible; and the temperature in the church during the tuning should be approximately the same as the temperature during the concert. It is important that the swell-boxes should have been left open: a modern organ has a gadget which automatically opens the boxes, but on an old organ the player has to remember to do it himself.) The orchestra will have several other difficulties to contend with. Cellists' spikes will squeak as they slither across the stone floor: someone should have reminded them to bring a small mat with them. The cellists will also be finding it uncomfortable to have to sit on the extreme edge of the sort of chair that slopes backwards because it has been shaped for stacking. But if you manage to discover one or two old-fashioned wooden chairs in the vestry they will probably be so rickety with age that they will collapse under the players' weight. The leading violinist may be asking for a cushion to make his chair the right height for playing, and the only available substitute will be a hassock, which will be much too high. The borrowed folding music-stands will have come apart during their journey in the boot of a car, and no one will have thought of tying a label to each half to make it easier to put them together. When the odd bits and pieces have at last been joined, enthusiastic helpers will seize a stand without waiting to see if it has been screwed up tightly enough; they will almost certainly hold it near the top instead of near the bottom, so that the metal joints will fall apart again, to the peril of anyone within reach. It is as well to be provided with sticking-plaster on these occasions. In fact, a conductor needs to bring a good deal of equipment in case of emergencies: the list includes spare conducting sticks; any available spare copies of the music; a tuning fork or pitch pipe; pencils and rubbers; several sheets of manuscript paper; scissors; adhesive tape; and a few medium-sized squares of cardboard which can be used either as a firm backing for flimsy orchestral parts or as tightly folded wedges to prevent a platform rocking to and fro on an uneven floor.

Tuning up. The orchestra must be given a chance to get in tune. You will have to persuade everyone to sit still and keep quiet. Don't try to shout at them through the pandemonium, as this will only increase their agitation: you must get them to be absolutely silent, and then say what you have to say in your normal speaking voice.

The final rehearsal. Every moment matters in a combined rehearsal. It is helpful to draw up a time-schedule for your own use, showing how long you intend to rehearse each item. You will not be able to keep to it, but it will be an approximate guide, and it will prevent you from spending far too long on the first piece and not having any time left for the last two or three items. At the very beginning of the rehearsal your time-schedule is likely to be upset by the arrival of a photographer from the local newspaper. It is no good losing your temper with him: he has to earn his living. Ask everyone to sing and play the first note of the first piece on a fortissimo-held pause, and bring them all in with a triumphant flourish of your stick. If the wretched man says that he also wants a close-up of the soloists, you must quickly gather them round you while you hold out your full score for them to look at: open it at random and point to a word at the top of a page as if you had only just noticed it for the first time. This never fails to satisfy a photographer, and with any luck he will clear off without having wasted more than three or four precious minutes. When you are able to begin rehearsing, try and go through every item in the right order, and let the singers practise standing up, finding the right note to start, and sitting down when it is over. If they sound husky owing to the inevitable coughs and colds of December, or owing to the embarrassment of hearing their own voices in church, you must encourage them without bullying them. But if they are careless about scooping or slowing-down in the wrong places you must be relentless. A sudden bellow of protest from a conductor, followed by a complete silence, can effectively cure any such self-indulgent faults. (This method, however, will not be successful if you have allowed yourself to get into the bad habit of shouting at them throughout their preliminary rehearsals, for they will be inured to the sound.) If the singers make mistakes owing to difficulties in the music, the awkward bit should be practised over and over again, until it feels safe. Never leave any insecure passage to 'come off all right on the night'. Try to end the rehearsal on time, as this is one of the things that matters. Thank them for their hard work; tell them that it is going to be a good performance; and remind them of the exact time when they should be in their places for the concert, ready to begin.

33. Performing in public

Waiting for the concert to begin. During the short breathing-space between the end of the combined rehearsal and the beginning of the performance you should try to escape from the people who go on asking questions all the time. Stop worrying about details of organization and allow yourself the luxury of thinking about the music. Eat as little as possible. It is unwise to accept any offer of alcohol: it can blunt your critical faculties and sap the foundation of the rhythm.

Last-minute crises. You should arrive at least fifteen minutes before the concert is due to begin, in case of unexpected crises such as snow-storms or traffic blocks. One of the worst things that can happen is an electricity cut. In a church concert it should be possible to borrow a few candles, but these will not give enough light for the players to see by, and the organ will be silent. The choir, however, will be able to sing unaccompanied carols by heart, and it is useful to be able to teach the audience some easy rounds, such as Exs. 31 and 35, to keep them happy until the lights come on again.

Going on to the platform. Before beginning the concert, you must be sure that all the performers are there. Try not to look too gloomy when you walk to the rostrum: you should give the members of the audience the impression that you are grateful to them for having come. If there is to be applause, do not make your bow as an isolated individual, but show with a gesture that it is the singers and players who are making the music. Refrain from tapping your stick on the edge of your music stand in imitation of a professional conductor seen on television: at an amateur concert this is seldom necessary, and it looks naïve as well as pretentious. All that is needed is the familiar 'attitude while waiting to begin' that was first mentioned on page 9, but you will have to hold it longer than usual until the audience has finished coughing.

Audiences. There is nothing terrifying about audiences. At first sight their faces will perhaps look blank, but this will either be because of the cold weather, or it may be just their natural expression. The fact that they have turned out on a winter's evening to sit on hard pews for an hour is sufficient proof that they are not hostile. And they are an important part of the occasion, for the give-and-take between performer and listener is one of the essential ingredients of music-making. You will know whether they are enjoying themselves, for their appreciation can make itself felt, especially in the short silence at the end of a piece. If your singers should happen to catch sight of a professional musician in the audience they will probably look alarmed. But he will be the least alarming person there, for he will be the only one who can recognize the phrasing that you are aiming at through all your difficulties.

Mistakes during the performance. In spite of all the trouble you have taken during the combined rehearsal, disasters may happen and the choir and orchestra may get out of time with each other. If the cellos come in two bars too soon, shout '*Wait!*' and hold your stick firmly in front of them while continuing to conduct the other players and singers with your left hand: at the cellists' real entry, give them a huge preparatory beat and say 'NOW!' Your singers may lose their nerve in an unaccompanied part-song that until then had always felt safe, and one of your strongest basses may come in at a fourth instead of a fifth below the tenors, dragging his neighbours with him. If you are a bass yourself you can sing the right note, fortissimo, while holding up both arms until the sound gets into focus. But if you are a soprano it will make it worse if you pipe up with the note an octave too high. You cannot be expected to guess when these calamities are likely to happen, but you can guard against them by going through

the programme with the organist some time before the final rehearsal, giving him copies of all the unaccompanied music, and
asking him to come to the rescue if needed.

Keeping calm. When things go badly, it is essential that you should
keep calm. Never allow yourself to feel angry about a mistake during
a performance: your singers and players will know what you are
thinking, and they will get more and more agitated. Remember that
the music will have a chance of righting itself if you can keep calm
enough for the rhythm to flow of its own accord. This is perhaps the
most difficult thing of all for a conductor to have to learn. And it is
not only when things go badly that one has to keep calm: it is just
as important when things are going well. A conductor must never get
over-excited: he has no right to be carried away by the beauty of the
music. Listeners in an audience can think profound thoughts and
feel moved to tears while the performance is going on: the conductor
has to apply his mind to what he is doing.

After the performance. When the concert is over you will be surrounded
by strangers wanting to talk to you. Keep them waiting while you
thank all the people who have helped you. Then deal with the
strangers: you will find that they all want information from you,
such as advice on the choice of a singing teacher for a granddaughter,
or of a composition teacher for a nephew. The music critic from the
county newspaper will ask you for historical details about items in the
programme: he will be waiting to write them down from your dicta-
tion. (This will teach you that on future occasions you must bring
typewritten programme notes for thrusting into his hand.) By the time
you have got rid of him you will discover to your dismay that you are
alone in the church, with the hired chairs to be stacked, and the
music-stands to be taken down, and the heavy brass lectern to be
moved back into position for the next morning's service. (And this
will teach you that organizing a concert means planning the rehearsals, the performance, and the clearing-up as one continuous
operation.)

The next day. The day after the concert is the right time for making a
list of all the things that went wrong with the organization. Give
this list to the secretary to read out at the next committee meeting,

and forget it. Then go through all the music, marking your scores, one after another, to remind yourself of what was too quick or too slow, and what was too loud or too soft, and where the phrasing was inadequate. Do not wait too long before holding this private 'post-mortem': the burden of recollection will wear off as the days pass by, and you may begin to wonder whether things really were as bad as they seemed. When you are trying to remember exactly what went wrong, you must not feel tempted to put all the blame on any individual singer or player. A conductor cannot shed his responsibility and divorce himself from his performers while the music is going on: they are all in it together, from the beginning to the end.

Listening to a play-back on a tape-recorder. It is not always possible to realize when one has hurried or dragged in a performance. A tape-recording will make this painfully clear. It will also point out some of the bad habits in conducting which the members of your choir may have been too polite to tell you about. You may think that you have cured yourself of singing while you are conducting, but the tape will present you with the unmistakable sound of a baritone warbling the tune an octave too low in a song intended for sopranos and altos. You may think that you no longer tap with your foot while conducting, but the play-back will faithfully reproduce a heavy thud at the beginning of each bar. You will possibly hear your voice saying 'AND' to supplement what should have been a silent preparatory beat. Or you may hear yourself grunting with effort at the entry of a new phrase, or drawing in your breath through your teeth. (Such faults, alas, are not easy to cure: it has taken me forty-five years to learn to stand still during rehearsals and performances.) Perhaps before long all learner-conductors will be able to possess their own video-cassettes, which will reproduce each gesture as well as each sound. We shall then know what our conducting looks like, and the sight may eventually teach us not to leap up and down with gawky gesticulations.

Ambitions for the future. A play-back is not always distressing all the way through: there may be frequent occasions when the singers' words are clear and the vitality of the rhythm is convincing. If, on the whole, your performance makes musical sense in spite of its shortcomings, you will want to go on to explore longer works, possibly combining with other choirs and with more experienced orchestral players.

The National Federation of Music Societies. This Federation helps amateur choral societies with their problems, by offering advice on concert-giving (including questions about performing rights), by making it possible for choirs to hire music from each other, by sending out catalogues of suitable choral music, and by organizing courses for conductors. (See page 156 for further information.)

PART XI

Competitive festivals

34. The syllabus

Competitive and non-competitive festivals. For many years people have argued about whether non-competitive music festivals are preferable to those that are competitive. In several counties the education authorities, looking askance at the money prizes and the medals, will support only the non-competitive work. But the opinion of most adjudicators is that there are no successful contests at the moment where there is not some degree of grading or where people do not know who has won. For an amateur choir-trainer, the best festivals, whether competitive or non-competitive, are those that encourage combined choral singing.

The British Federation of Music Festivals. If your choir wants to enter for a festival, you should write to the British Federation of Music Festivals for advice. (See page 155.) They will send you a list of the hundreds of affiliated festivals throughout the country, with the names and addresses of the honorary secretaries, and the dates when the local festivals are being held. The Federation's description of a Combined Choir Festival is 'one where various choirs train in their own districts and then come together for a day of combined rehearsal, with a performance in the evening. The range of size is considerable: the largest engages a London orchestra for three days and puts on magnificent concerts: the smallest combines three village choirs.'

Test pieces in the syllabus. If the test pieces are from one of the great choral masterpieces of the last four hundred years, including those of today, you should be able to keep your choir thoroughly happy during months of preliminary rehearsals. But if the work is one that you dislike, it would be wise to decide not to enter your choir for that year. Your singers may be disappointed, but you should never forget that you can only be of use to them if your heart is in what you are doing. A professional conductor may have to earn his living on works that he hates, until he is sufficiently in demand to be able to say 'no'. It is the amateur conductor's privilege to be able to choose the music he works at. I know that there are people who disagree with this: they believe that one has a duty to teach one's choir what is described as 'the accepted standard repertory'. But this attitude, which is verging on conscription, leads to a distressing increase in the number of well-meaning, dull, and unwanted performances. There is far too much music in existence for any amateur conductor to get to know more than a tiny proportion of it, and it would be a wicked waste of opportunity not to concentrate on what you passionately want to do, if it is technically suitable for your singers.

'Own choice' pieces. One of the items on the syllabus will be an 'own choice'. This should be in complete contrast to the test piece: in a different mood, style, speed, key, and time signature. If the test piece is with accompaniment, it would be as well to have your own choice unaccompanied.

The official accompanist. The syllabus will mention if you are allowed to take your own accompanist with you. You will have to decide whether your pianist is good enough: if you have any doubts, it would be better to arrange for the choir to sing with the official accompanist. He will be a skilled player, with many years' experience in guessing the meaning of the obscure hesitations of an anxious conductor.

'Over'-rehearsing. Your choir is not likely to complain of boredom if you avoid any routine repetition of the pieces you are working at. 'Over'-rehearsed means 'badly' rehearsed. Allow plenty of time for learning the works: get them by heart, and then put them aside for two or three weeks while you teach the choir something quite different. Then revise them, and try and arrange for a small informal audience to hear them several days before the competition. This will give you a final chance to polish any details that may have suffered owing to the nervous strain of performing in front of listeners.

35. Nerves

Varying effects of nervousness. Amateur conductors, when faced with the ordeal of performing in public, are sometimes seized with a false jauntiness which makes them hurry through each phrase with jittery staccato gestures. Others feel numbed with a dread that has an almost paralysing effect on their movements, so that they doubt if they will be able to raise their arms for a preparatory beat. And many people are frightened of forgetting what they have memorized, with the result that they think about themselves instead of the music. A textbook is supposed to offer advice, but as no two individuals ever feel nervous in quite the same way, only the most general guidance is possible, such as the warnings about eating and drinking mentioned in Chapter 33. Try not to get over-tired before the performance begins. This may be difficult, especially after a hard day's work and a crowded journey during the rush-hour. But you can at any rate plan your work so that you do not have to stay up very late the night before the performance. (A conductor who boasts of having learnt his score until three in the morning is giving himself away: there is no virtue in working for long hours through the night.) Your friends will say: 'Stop worrying, and relax.' But it may be some time before you can discover your own most suitable method for trying to reduce the tension.

Some fallacies about nerves before a performance. It would be comforting to be able to believe that nervous anxiety becomes less of a problem with each public performance. But this is not so. There are distinguished professional conductors who still feel sick five minutes before they have to appear on the platform. It is a fallacy, however, to suppose that a conductor is insensitive if he never feels nervous during the half-hour before a performance: the music will not suffer just because he has managed to keep calm.

Confidence. The greatest help to a nervous conductor is knowing his score thoroughly: this will give him the sort of confidence that is a necessary part of conducting. The word 'confident' has been defined as 'self-reliant', but no conductor worth listening to is self-reliant: the best musicians are aware of their own inadequacies. If you are able to feel confident while conducting at your first competitive festival it will be because you are relying not only on the singers but also on the composer. The music itself can cure your jittery nerves or your lapses of memory, for it is a continuous whole, from the first note to the last. If you rely on the flow of the rhythm it will save you.

Warnings about adjudicators. Competitive festivals are more nerve-racking than concerts. The audience consists of fellow-victims who are waiting their turn to walk up the steep, slippery steps and to stand in straight rows in the middle of the immense platform. An unnatural hush will hang over the proceedings: when your turn comes you must let the choir break through the unreality and sing with abandon. It is worth realizing that the adjudicator will be having just as difficult a task as everyone else. (As an ex-adjudicator, I can remember the agony of having to mark thirty-nine vocal quartets who all sang 'Love is *meant* to make us glad' in exactly the same way.) The following warnings may prove useful to your singers:

(1) When you are on the platform, about to begin, the adjudicator will say: 'Just wait a minute, would you,' while he writes his criticism of the previous choir. You will be kept standing for three or four minutes, in a deadly silence, while the two hundred competitors in the audience stare at your unfortunate singers. Warn them beforehand that this may happen, and suggest that they should find something quite different to think about, such as the next day's shopping list, or plans for the next summer's holiday. When the adjudicator finally rings his bell for you to begin, catch the eye of your singers as you raise your arms, and silently whisper an appropriate comment such as: 'At *last*!' This will help them to relax the muscles round their mouths, and their faces will once more become instruments for making music.

(2) When you are beginning the second verse of the test piece the adjudicator may suddenly ring his bell, as a signal for 'Stop: that's enough!' This can upset choirs so much that they are often unable to give an adequate performance of their next song.

(3) In the brief interval between your two items you may notice that the adjudicator is scowling heavily, with a look of desperation on his face. This may have nothing to do with the singing: he will probably have glanced at his watch and will have realized that he is ten minutes behind his time-schedule, with no chance of catching up.

36.   Criticism and encouragement

Criticism as a stimulating experience. The adjudicator's remarks about
your performance will have to be brief, but if he is good at his job
his advice will be practical. And the remarks will not just be 'fault-
finding', for that is only one of the meanings of the word criticism.
A true critic is 'able to discern'. Your adjudicator may be able to
give you a glimpse of the lost opportunities in your performance,
and this kind of criticism can be a stimulating experience.

Interpretation. In old-fashioned competitive festivals the adjudicator
was supposed to give so many marks for 'accuracy' and so many for
'interpretation'. I always found this puzzling, because it was difficult
to know where the one began and the other ended. From the point
of view of an amateur choir-trainer, a 'good interpretation' is a
performance that is lively, sensitive, and intelligent enough to allow
the music to speak for itself.

'Right' or 'wrong' interpretation can be a matter of opinion. If a living
composer is listening to a performance of his music he can tell us
whether it sounds right or not. But if the composer of the test piece
for a competitive festival has been dead for over two hundred years,
the decision about whether an interpretation is right or wrong will
be a matter of opinion. Ideas about performing early music have
altered a great deal during the last half century. When your adjudicator gives you poor marks for your Bach chorale, telling you that
it should have been twice as slow, you must not despair. Adjudicators
are sometimes old, and even if they are not old in years they may
still be accepting unquestioningly the lessons they learnt from their
teachers. It is no use protesting, and quoting any of the recently
published information about baroque music mentioned in Chapter
21. That is not your job. It is your job to listen to the Bach performances that thrill you, and to grasp hold of what sounds convincing. Each generation has to bring Bach's music to life in its own
way. And the people who organize the competitive festivals know
this. A recent 'Year Book' of the British Federation of Music
Festivals quotes William Plomer's wise saying: 'What was good
enough for our predecessors can never be good enough for us, because
we live under different conditions and we are very different people.'

Success. It will be immensely encouraging for your singers if they manage to win their competition. But if the local music critic writes: 'It was the best performance of that madrigal I have ever heard,' you should realize that he may have heard it only once before in his life, sung by a choir even less experienced than your own.

Standards. When my father conducted amateur choirs he used to warn them to avoid getting to a certain standard and then settling down and never getting any further. That was sixty years ago, but the warning is still needed today.

37. Singing with combined choirs under an experienced conductor

The transformation in choral singing when small choirs are combined into one large chorus. It is the combined rehearsal that makes it worth while going in for a competitive festival. A miraculous change comes over the singing. Your three husky tenors, when surrounded by thirty or forty other tenors, will sing as they have never sung before. The dozens of small choirs, which have sounded scared throughout the day, will throw aside all caution. High notes will sound clear and effortless. Everyone will have enough breath for sustaining the long-drawn-out pianissimo passages. Each crescendo will mount up with a thrilling intensity, and there will be a terrific attack on each *ff* entry. Even the technically difficult runs will sound brilliant. And there will be an astonishing quality of warmth and lyrical beauty in the singing which none of the choir-trainers will have heard at any of their preliminary rehearsals.

Learning from watching a good conductor. You should ask permission to sit with your choir throughout the combined rehearsal and performance, as you can learn so much from watching a good conductor rehearsing the music that you have tried to conduct yourself. You will be amazed to see how he controls everything without making any huge gestures. He will seem to be doing very little, yet he will be bringing in each entry with a clear indication of what is wanted. His economical movements at a crescendo or a rallentando will be easy to follow, and you will always know what he is asking you to do, before it actually happens. The pauses which occur at the end of each line of a chorale will never be static: they will be conveyed as a prolonged rubato, without interrupting the flow of the music. And the silences between the sections of the work will never seem like empty gaps that need joining up: they will be part of the music, and they will always last for exactly the right length of time. This is what people mean when they talk about the wonderful 'timing' of a performance. There can never be any words to describe the sense of wholeness in this continuity, because it is something that only happens in music, and it needs music to express it. You cannot hope to imitate what a great conductor does, but having once rehearsed under him you will know what you will be aiming at in the future.

Performing with professionals. The overwhelming experience of performing with good professional soloists and a good professional orchestra will convince you that it is worth struggling with all the difficulties mentioned in the previous chapters if there is to be a chance of going on with that sort of combined music-making. And it is encouraging to know that great professional conductors will always need the help of amateur choruses who can phrase like musicians.

PART XII

Preparing works for combined performance

38.   Choruses from Purcell's *Dido and Aeneas*

The following suggestions are not concerned with the problems of a stage production: they are meant for teaching the notes of some of the choruses in preparation for a concert performance. Begin by telling your singers the story. If they are using vocal scores they can get to know the whole work. (See page 150 for details of editions.) If they are singing from chorus copies you should offer to lend them a vocal score or a libretto to read. At rehearsals, you should always include the cues that lead into the choruses, so that no one has any doubts about where to come in.

In the first scene, the chorus represents the courtiers, who are enthusiastic about the prospects of a royal wedding between Queen Dido and Prince Aeneas.

Ex. 46

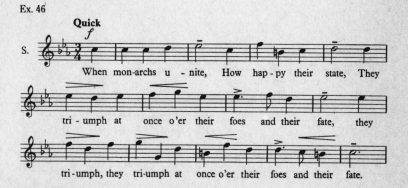

When monarchs unite (Ex. 46). The energy in the singing must not be allowed to sound jerky: sustain the words 'unite', 'state', and 'fate' as long as possible. Roll the 'r' in 'triumph', and then relax for the second syllable, to give a sense of well-being: if the 'm' is thin-lipped it will sound peevish.

Ex. 47

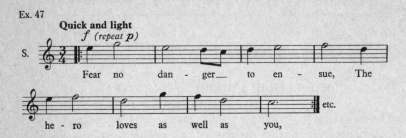

Fear no danger (Ex. 47). This can feel uncomfortably high for amateur sopranos: in Purcell's time the pitch would have been a whole tone lower. Help them by encouraging the other voices to sing their words very clearly, so that the soprano line can float through the consonants. Avoid putting an unwanted accent on the syncopated minim just because it is a longer note than the crotchet. This is a dancing rhythm, like so many of Purcell's songs. (In the libretto, a stage direction after 'Fear no danger' says: 'Dance this Chorus.') There is no need for a conductor to know the steps and figures of a Purcell dance, but he must be sensitive to the rhythm and he must be able to convey it to his singers so that they make it feel like a dance.

Ex. 48

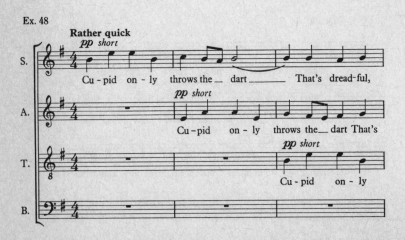

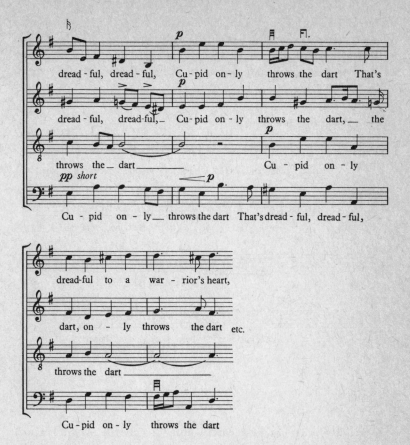

Cupid only throws the dart (Ex. 48). Here the courtiers are turning to each other and whispering among themselves: the polyphonic entries give the impression of conversation in an aside. One can imagine their shrugging shoulders and their confidential smiles at each repetition of the ironic word 'dreadful'. These gestures are easy on the stage: in a concert version they have to be implied in the characterization of the singing.

To the hills and the vales (Ex. 49). The exhilarating mood of this chorus must not tempt you to begin it too quickly: the speed is set by the dotted rhythm of the ninth bar. In this bar the marked repetition of the 'i' in 'triumphs' can be attacked with a slight 'h'. At the beginning of bar 10, the crotchet must move smoothly to the second syllable of the word, so that its meaning is not lost. (This applies to all similar passages in baroque music where there are many short notes to one syllable of a word.)

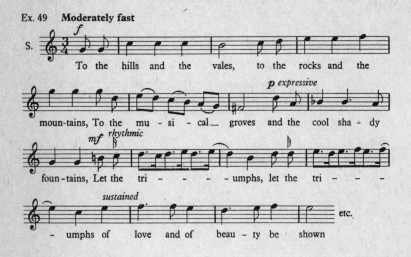

The scene changes to a cave where the chorus of witches are plotting ruin for Dido.

Harm's our delight (Ex. 50). The witches must sound evil. But this does not mean that their singing should be ugly. Remind your choir of Mozart's advice when he said that 'passions must never be expressed in such a way as to excite disgust, and music must never cease to be music'. Help the singers to convey the mood by exaggerating the stressed words: the 'm' of 'mischief' can be nasal in its contempt, and the 'k' of 'skill' should cut like a knife.

Ho ho ho! (Ex. 51). Teach it slowly and legato to 'la la la'. Let the singers memorize the pattern of notes as you increase the speed from andante to allegretto. Then take it presto to 'ho'. Avoid the diphthong 'hoh-oo'. The vowel sound can be nearer to the 'o' in 'hot', as this is more of a chuckle.

In our deep-vaulted cell (Ex. 52). Try the echo with a subconductor and a few singers in the next room: if the door is shut they need not sing too softly. Don't worry if there is a slight delay, as this is appropriate for the sense of distance, and echoes give the impression of getting slower as well as softer. The singing must be sustained throughout, so that it suggests the resonance of a cave. The word 'dreadful' should sound horror-struck, as if the witches were appalled by the spell they were casting.

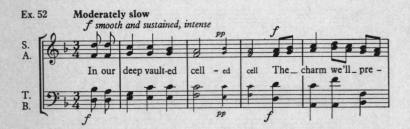

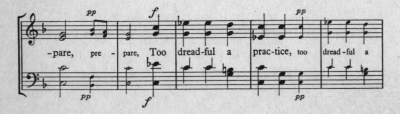

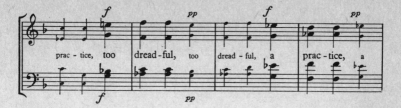

The scene changes to a grove of trees, and the singers are again representing the courtiers.

Thanks to these lonesome vales (Ex. 53). This is another dance tune. Guard against a 'refined' tone: the first word must not sound like 'thenks'.

Ex. 53   **Graceful**

Haste, haste to town (Ex. 54). A sudden rain-storm sends the courtiers hurrying for shelter. The mood of the music is bustling and anxious, which is just what amateur choirs so often sound like when one doesn't want them to. Here, however, the bustle and anxiety must be founded on accurately placed notes and controlled rhythm.

The scene changes to the quay-side: the chorus of sailors are making ready to leave.

Ex. 55

Come away, fellow sailors (Ex. 55). The song is energetically cheerful. When the singers have learnt it up to time you can conduct it in the flexible kind of three-in-a-bar which has a minim beat followed by a crotchet. Change to a legato one-in-a-bar for the smoothly ironical 'silence their mourning with vows of returning'. Then pick up the rhythm with three precise crotchet beats to each bar for the cynical aside about 'never intending to visit them more'.

Destruction's our delight (Ex. 56). The witches come back for another chorus, gloating over the success of their evil plot. Their singing should sound fierce.

Great minds against themselves conspire (Ex. 57a). The mood here is a complete contrast: it is like the chorus in a Greek drama. The singers are standing aside from the action of the opera and commenting on it. Their first utterance should sound vast and all-embracing. The beautifully expressive phrase 'And shun the cure they most desire' (Ex. 57b) is quiet, but it should not be sung sweetly: it is weighed down by the dark and bitter tragedy of all the marriages that have ever gone wrong.

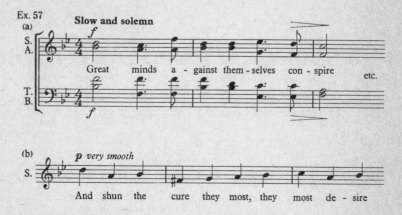

Ex. 57

With drooping wings (Ex. 58a). This final chorus can be difficult to start, because it joins the last bar of Dido's Lament, and singers are often overcome by their emotion. Tell them to swallow and relax just before coming in. And they need not pronounce their first consonant very distinctly. At the words 'soft, soft' (Ex. 58b), each repetition should be phrased with a diminuendo, and the second note should be only a quaver in length, with a quaver's worth of silence after it.

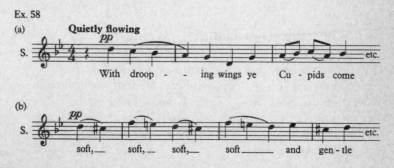

Ex. 58

The words 'never, never' (Ex. 58c) are not easy to get right: one is tempted to do too much with them, and the silences get longer and longer and the beats get slower and slower. When you are working at this alone, between choir practices, you may find it easier if you listen to the harmonies in your mind's ear as if they were legato minims. Then let them lift into silence, and they will keep their continuity. This will help you to give the singers a true rubato.

39. Choruses from Handel's *L'Allegro*

This secular oratorio has some of the best tunes that Handel ever wrote. There are plenty of opportunities for characterization in the contrasting choruses for *L'Allegro* (Cheerfulness) and *Il Penseroso* (Pensiveness). The following half-dozen extracts can give only a glimpse of the many possibilities of the work. (See page 150 for editions that are available.)

Haste thee, nymph (Ex. 59a). The cheerful opening bar should not be too staccato or it will sound clipped and prickly: let the singers hold the word 'nymph' for its full length and then bring off the 'mph' on the crotchet rest. Avoid an unwanted first-beat accent at the end of 'Jollity'. At the word 'derides', there can be an audible 'h' for each energetic quaver, as in the 'ha ha ha' of 'laughter' and the 'ho ho ho' of 'holding'. The sopranos must relax their jaws for the high repeated 'laughter' of bars 11 and 12 or it will turn into a hard-edged cackle. In Ex. 59b the basses' repeated crotchets will sound intolerably ponderous if they are sung at a level forte: the editorial suggestion of a gradual crescendo helps to shape the phrase.

Ex. 59

Come and trip it (Ex. 60). The lilting rhythm needs the unevenly divided beat (DOWN-down, UP-up) which always suits the flow of a ⁶⁄₈ dance at this speed. The first word, 'Come,' must sound like a

happy invitation. (I used to suggest to my choirs that they should
think of the person they would most like to see coming in at the door
while they sang it.) If the sentence is phrased as if it were meant, it
will escape the all-too-frequent distortion of 'Cahm, and tree-ee-eep
it'. A rolled 'r' in 'trip' helps to lighten the repeated phrase in bars 9
and 10. You may find that the singers will come in late here, having
taken too long over the quaver rests: if this happens, you should
beware of the temptation to beat out their notes for them (ONE TWO
stop FOUR FIVE stop) as this utterly destroys the feel of the dance.
The phrasing for the word 'go' in bars 11 and 12 is an editorial
suggestion. Most editions of eighteenth-century choral music still
show a conventional slur over any group of notes that is to be sung
to one syllable. This can be confusing, as it could look as if the whole
passage were meant to be sung legato. If you are faced with this
problem of conventional slurs in any editions you are using, you will
have to decide for yourself about each phrase, according to its shape
and meaning.

Ex. 60

Join with thee calm Peace and Quiet (Ex. 61). Here the mood changes to
Pensiveness. The music must be very smooth. The quaver rest after
'thee' must not interrupt the meaning of the sentence. Let them try
singing it once with a dotted crotchet on 'thee' so that they can feel
the underlying continuity: then lift it, with the phrasing that Handel

has asked for. In the corresponding place at 'Spare Fast that oft with gods doth diet' it is important that the singers should not take a new breath in the rest, as this could result in an unwanted stress on 'with'.

Ex. 61

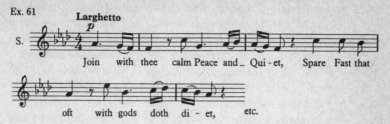

And young and old come forth to play (Ex. 62a). This characteristic rhythm for Cheerfulness is a dancing $\frac{12}{8}$: it is an example of the 'inequality' mentioned on page 77.

Ex. 62
(a)

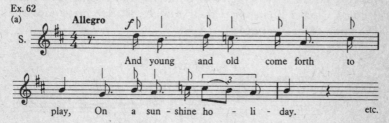

Ex. 62b shows a difficult entry after a silent first beat. If you give too energetic a down-beat in this silence and then try to bring them in with a rigid indication it will make them tighten their necks. This will close up the back of their throats, and the A will come out as a constricted screech. Try holding the semibreve at the end of the previous sentence as if it were a pause. Then, instead of beating for the crotchet rest, *relax* into it, and you will be able to move easily into a legato gesture for the singers' entry. *Don't look worried.* Imagine the sound that you are hoping to hear, and look gratefully at the sopranos.

(b)

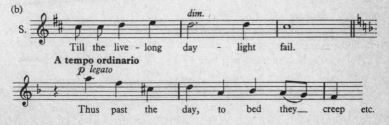

Populous cities please us then (Ex. 63a). This exhilarating chorus begins with the six bars introduction for solo bass shown in Ex. 63a. Let your chorus basses have the pleasure of singing this at your preliminary rehearsals, but warn them that they will be having six bars rest on the day of the performance. (And make them write a reminder of this in their copies, or you will hear your most robust baritone coming in with an explosive 'POP' in front of the audience.) When you first teach the notes of this chorus, your whole choir can practise these six bars in unison, as an exercise in making the 'zzz' of 'busy' sound like a swarm of bees. In the fifth bar they can experiment with pronouncing the word 'hum' as if it were 'hmmm'; and let them sing the word with as much tone as they can. The contrasting middle section of the chorus, at Ex. 63b, should, if possible, be sung by a semi-chorus. It must not sound unhappy: remind them that it is still in the character of *L'Allegro*. And it must not sound 'refained': make them open their mouths if they lapse into the affectation of 'brayeet ayees'.

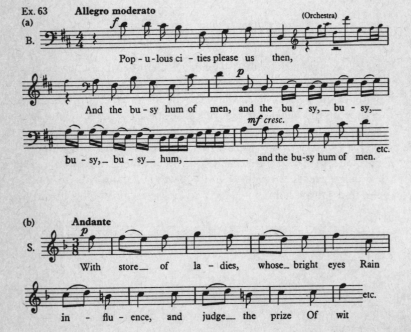

Ex. 64

A tempo ordinario

A.

These plea - sures, Me - lan - cho - ly, give, *etc.*

T.

And we with thee will choose to live _____

Pft. reduction

etc.

These pleasures, Melancholy, give (Ex. 64). The three bars shown in Ex. 64 are the opening of a long fugue in the mood of Pensiveness. Handel's choral fugues need a great deal of hard work at rehearsals to prevent them sounding dull. Each vocal line should be practised in turn, over the instrumental bass. The words, as always, should be phrased according to their meaning, and should never be neglected because of the complexity of the counterpoint. In the third bar of Ex. 64, for instance, the altos must not be allowed to dig themselves in with a first-beat accent on a weak syllable: in the orchestra the second violins, who are doubling the altos' tune, play their quaver D tied to the previous crotchet, which tells us the phrasing that Handel had in his mind. (See the piano reduction in Ex. 64.) The texture in a choral fugue will always sound stodgy if all the voices sing equally loudly all the time. To avoid this stodginess, you can let the main subject sound more important than anything else, whenever it occurs. (In Ex. 64, this is the alto line.) The next in importance is the counter-subject, which can be quieter than the main subject. (In Ex. 64, this is the tenor line.) When any of the voices are not singing either of these themes they are given short fragments which repeat some of the words that have already been sung, over and over again. These background phrases should be quieter than the counter-subject. If they push their way to the forefront, the singers on the main theme will have to bellow to keep up their importance. And then the phrasing will be lost, and everything will sound heavy and lifeless. But if you can keep the right balance, the texture will be clear.

40. Choruses from Britten's *Rejoice in the Lamb*

Amateur choir-trainers are sometimes reluctant to venture on per-forming twentieth-century music: they are scared of its strange sounds. New music by a good composer is sure to sound unexpected at a first hearing, because his mind will have stretched further than the rest of us are able to reach. We cannot hope to catch up with him in invention, but as soon as his work is available in print we can begin to learn it, and we can go on practising until it becomes familiar to us: it will then sound simple and inevitable. One of the advantages of working at music by a twentieth-century composer is that every detail in the printed copy is authentic. There is no need for an editor to add his suggestions for performance: each slur and dynamic and metronome mark is the composer's own request.

If you want to work at Britten's cantata *Rejoice in the Lamb* you will be able to listen to his own recording before you memorize the score. Let your singers hear the record at their first rehearsal, while they follow it in their copies. (See page 150 for details of publication.) The organ part is difficult to play on the piano, and you will need an experienced accompanist for your preliminary rehearsals. Some of the passages are easier with two players, and many of the low sustained notes written for organ pedals will have to be repeated on the piano before the sound dies away.

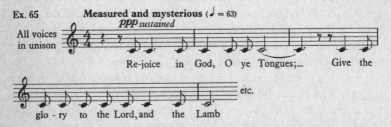

Rejoice in God, O ye Tongues (Ex. 65). The mysterious sound of this chanting must be accurate in its timing, but it must give the impression of a *senza misura* freedom, as in plainsong. This can only be achieved after a good deal of practice in phrasing the words according to their meaning. The repeated C is a true unison, with the tenors and basses at the same level as the sopranos and altos, instead of at the usual lower octave: the basses will need to sing very lightly to blend with the other hushed voices. The 's' of 'Tongues' belongs to the quaver rest that follows the tied note. The next quaver rest is for a new breath. Owing to the quiet, sustained mood of the music your singers may possibly be late on their word 'Give'. This is a very frequent fault in choral singing whenever there is an entry immediately after a silent beat. A rest before such an entry should never be thought of as a signal for waiting: it is an invitation to sing.

Let Nimrod the mighty hunter (Ex. 66.) This chorus is not nearly as difficult as it looks. The rhythm of the accompaniment, with its

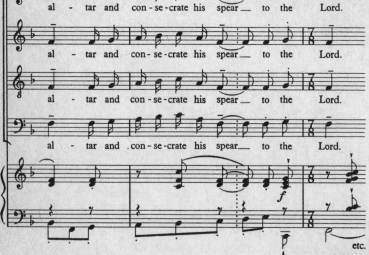

pattern of cha|um-cha um-cha:um-cha-cha is easy to memorize, and the singers can try tapping it with their hands on their laps: right| *left*-right *left*-right : *left*-right-right. When you want them to begin practising the tune slowly, you can beat the ⁷⁄₈ in quavers: up |*down*-down *in*-in:*out*-out-up. As soon as they are able to sing it quickly you will find the seven beats in a bar too fussy. You should then follow the indication written above the stave at the beginning of Ex. 66, beating the ⁷⁄₈ with two crotchets followed by an unevenly divided dotted crotchet: up|DOWN IN:OUT-up. The rhythm of the dotted crotchet at the end of the ⁷⁄₈ bar makes it easy to go straight into the ⁶⁄₈ at bar 5. Be careful not to make too large a gesture when you change to ⁶⁄₈ or the choir will come in *ff* instead of *pp*. You will find that it helps the singers if they memorize this chorus while they are learning it. Having mastered Nimrod, let them go on to Ishmail, and get this new bit by heart before attempting Balaam. And let them link up Nimrod, Ishmail, and Balaam before going on to Daniel. (Choirs never object to working thoroughly hard at a lively piece of music when there is a chance of getting it right: the thing that depresses them is muddling through, week after week.)

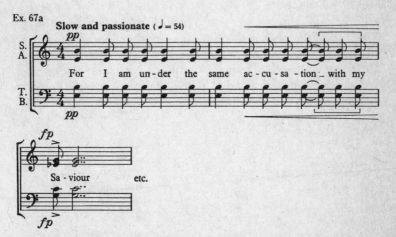

For I am under the same accusation (Ex. 67a). The declamation, as in Ex. 65, must be accurately timed while feeling free. The composer's request that the singing should be passionate will prevent the quiet tone from sounding dreary, and it will make it easier to get the bare fifth in tune. At the lamenting phrase 'For Silly fellow!' (Ex. 67b) the singers may have difficulty in finding the right notes. The held low C of the accompaniment will help them, for they will be able to listen to each melodic interval above it, in the same sort of way that Indian musicians hear their strange microtonal intervals in relation to a repeated pedal note. When you first begin working at Ex. 67b, take it quietly, and let the sopranos sing in unison with the altos while the tenors sing in unison with the basses. This will make it possible for them to repeat it as often as they need to, without becoming exhausted. As soon as they have learnt the pattern of the phrase securely, you will be able to let them sing it forte at the right octave.

For I am in twelve Hardships (Ex. 68). This beautiful sentence, with its entries in canon, must be as sustained as possible. Let the choir sing through each singable consonant: l, m, n, th, and v. The sopranos will have no difficulty in coming in very quietly on such a low first note, but you may have to help the altos to get a true pianissimo at this warm level of their voices. The crescendo should rise very gradually towards the tremendous intensity of the climax.

For the instruments are by their rhimes (Ex. 69). The rhythm is one in a bar: the entries at the half bar must be practised until they are clear, confident, and in time. Notice the accent on the word 'are' in the first phrase: the verb is used in the sense of 'exist'. The sforzando on 'rhimes', with its long diminuendo, should sound like the stroke of a bell that fades into silence. When the quick rhymes follow with their exciting emphasis, you must try not to get over-excited yourself: there is a long way to go before the climax, and if you lash out with your arms the singers will sharpen and force their tone.

Ex. 69

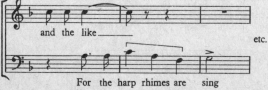

Ex. 70a

Hallelujah (Ex. 70a). The rhythm is one of Britten's many legacies from Purcell. He suggests that it should be sung approximately as a quintuplet and if your choir can phrase it instinctively they will be able to sing the chorus as it should be sung. Let them practise it in unison to the sopranos' opening phrase of 'Hallelujah, Hallelujah', sung by heart. When this feels effortless, they can go on. If they lose the rhythm while trying to phrase their words over the bar-line, as in 'the artist inimitable', they should go back to that first Hallelujah to remind themselves of how easy it is. The mood of the final pianissimo entries at Ex. 70b must be happy: this will enable the choir to keep in tune throughout the quiet rallentando at the end. When Britten was rehearsing this chorus with the Purcell Singers for his recording of the work, he told them that the rhythm should sound 'casual'. This may seem a strange word for a composer to use when conducting his own music. But it is the right word to describe the ease that he was asking for. And this ease is something that an amateur choir can achieve.

Ex. 70b

Conclusion

There can be no satisfactory conclusion to a textbook for learners, because the learning goes on all the time. Even a great conductor will admit after a superb performance that 'it's coming, but there's still a long way to go'.

If you are hoping to continue learning conducting, the long way that you still have to go may possibly lead you to a day when you will no longer be considered an amateur because you will be paid for the job. People sometimes say that it is a mistake for a professional conductor to have begun his training by working with amateurs. I find it impossible to agree. If you begin on beginners you will learn from your own mistakes: if you begin on professionals your mistakes will be ignored and it may be difficult for you to know what you have done wrong. There can be no short-cut to the experience of learning by trial and error.

It is true that it is not easy to change suddenly from conducting amateurs to conducting professionals. There are various things that professional singers and players object to: they dislike unnecessarily large preparatory beats, and they hate audible reminders of the approach of a repeat, or of a new dynamic, or of a change of key signature. But when you have adjusted yourself to the standards of such a different way of life you will find that your chief difficulty will be to keep calm when the music you are conducting sounds more beautiful than you had ever imagined it could sound.

The main essentials are the same in conducting amateurs and conducting professionals. And any professional singer or player would agree that the three golden rules apply to *all* conductors: learn your score thoroughly, don't talk too much, and listen to what you are hearing.

Notes on the music examples

Most of the unison songs (Exs. 1–15) and the rounds and canons (Exs. 16–42) are to be found in the collections mentioned in the first paragraph of *Suggestions for suitable music* on page 151. (There is no volume published that contains *all* the rounds one would like to sing.)

Exs. 43–5 are from *Invitation to Madrigals*, Books 1 and 2, edited by Thurston Dart, published by Stainer and Bell. (See paragraph 3 of *Suggestions for suitable music*.)

There are several editions of Purcell's *Dido and Aeneas*:

(a) edited by Benjamin Britten and Imogen Holst, published by Boosey and Hawkes
(b) edited by Margaret Laurie and Thurston Dart, published by Novello
(c) edited by Edward J. Dent, published by the Oxford University Press, with an alternative version for sopranos and altos.

Exs. 46–58 are taken from the Boosey and Hawkes edition.

Handel's *L'Allegro* is published by Novello (edited by W. H. Monk). There is also a shortened version arranged for sopranos and altos by Imogen Holst, published by Curwen (Curwen-Faber, available from Faber Music). Exs. 59–64 are adapted from the Curwen-Faber edition.

Britten's *Rejoice in the Lamb* (Exs. 65–70) is published by Boosey and Hawkes.

For addresses of publishers, see page 154.

Suggestions for further reading

CONDUCTING AND CHOIR TRAINING

A Handbook on the Technique of Conducting, Adrian C. Boult (Hall; reissued by Paterson's Publications).
The Fundamentals of Singing, Charles Kennedy Scott (Cassell).
Choral Conducting, Archibald T. Davison (Harvard; Oxford University Press).

SIGHT-READING AND RUDIMENTS

Learn to read music, Howard Shanet (Faber and Faber).
An A.B.C. of Music, Imogen Holst (Oxford University Press).

EDITING

Editions and Musicians, Walter Emery (Novello).

Editing Early Music, produced jointly by Novello, Oxford University Press, and Stainer and Bell.

The Interpretation of Music, Thurston Dart (Hutchinson University Library).

The Interpretation of Early Music, Robert Donington (Faber and Faber). This reference volume, available in libraries, gives many details of gracing and inequality, etc.

MUSIC COPYING

Musical Handwriting, Archibald Jacob (Oxford University Press).

Hart's Rules for Compositors (Oxford University Press). This gives information about hyphens in the division of words (including Latin), which is useful when copying chorus parts.

SCORE-READING AND ORCHESTRATION

How to read a score, Gordon Jacob (Boosey and Hawkes).

Score Reading; Book IV, Oratorios, Roger Fiske (Oxford University Press).

Orchestration, Walter Piston (Gollancz).

Flute Technique, Oboe Technique, Clarinet Technique, etc. (Oxford University Press). Short booklets by experts, giving clear details of how each instrument is played.

Suggestions for suitable music for amateur choirs

UNISON SONGS, FOLK-SONGS, AND ROUNDS

The Oxford Song Book, Vol. II, collected and arranged by Thomas Wood (Oxford University Press).

Singing for Pleasure, edited by Imogen Holst (Oxford University Press). Intended for equal voices, but the thirty rounds can be sung by mixed voices.

Twice 44 Sociable Songs, collected and arranged by Geoffrey Shaw (Boosey and Hawkes).

The Oxford Book of Carols, edited by Percy Dearmer, R. Vaughan Williams, and Martin Shaw (Oxford University Press).

The Penguin Book of English Folk Songs, edited by R. Vaughan Williams and A. L. Lloyd (Penguin Books).

A Selection of Folk-Songs arranged by Cecil J. Sharp, R. Vaughan Williams, and others (Novello).

North Countrie Folk Songs, edited and arranged by W. G. Whittaker (Curwen-Faber, from Faber Music).

SIGHT-SINGING

The Folk-Song Sight Singing Series, Books 1–7, compiled and edited by E. Crowe, A. Lawton, and W. G. Whittaker (Oxford University Press).
A collection of folk tunes of many countries. The tunes are graded: Book 1 is easy enough for beginners.
100 Tunes for Sight-Singing in the bass clef, compiled by C. S. Lang (Novello).

MADRIGALS, PART-SONGS, ANTHEMS, AND MOTETS

Invitation to Madrigals, edited by Thurston Dart; Vol. 1, S.A.B.; Vol. 2, S.A.T.B.; Vol. 3, S.S.A. (Stainer and Bell). The graded selections in these small books have admirable footnotes giving practical advice to singers and conductors.

It would fill too many pages to mention the hundreds of madrigals and part-songs, suitable for amateur choirs, that are published separately. The firms whose addresses are given below will send out their catalogues of choral music. Many sixteenth-century English madrigals and anthems are published by Stainer and Bell and the Oxford University Press; folk-song settings for unaccompanied voices are also published by these two firms, and by Curwen-Roberton, Boosey and Hawkes, and several other companies. Chester's catalogue contains a large number of Latin motets by the great composers of the sixteenth century. Novello and Co. publish many eighteenth- and nineteenth-century part-songs, and also Bach chorales.

Choral Works

The National Federation of Music Societies (see address on page 156) publish a 'Catalogue of Choral Works'. For advice about twentieth-century choral works, write to The Standing Conference for Amateur Music (see address for the National Council of Social Service). They supply a 'List of Recommended Modern Choral Music'.

Useful Information

EQUIPMENT

A good retail music shop in a city or a large town should stock all the equipment you are likely to need. It is worth making a journey to find out what is available, as this may save you from the frustration of having to work with inadequate materials.

Sticks will probably be too long, and will need shortening. You should ask to be shown an example of the right length, so that you can test the balance while you are still in the shop.

Baton cases for protecting your sticks are made of thin cardboard, shaped like a cylinder. They are cheap to buy and light to carry.

Tuning forks are available in A or C.

Pitch pipes, with the single note A, are suitable for each member of the choir to possess. Chromatic pipes, which can be quickly adjusted to any of the twelve levels of pitch within an octave, are much more expensive. Conductors sometimes find them useful for giving the note for unaccompanied singing: they should be blown as quietly as possible.

Metronomes that tick should not be used while a choir is singing, but, as mentioned on page 22, they can be useful to a conductor who is practising in solitude. They must always be placed on a perfectly horizontal flat surface. Unfortunately they are expensive to buy. Second-hand metronomes are sometimes unreliable. A small, cheap 'tape' metronome, which swings like a pendulum while held in one hand, can show the speed of a given metronome mark.

Manuscript paper is sold at nearly all music shops, and also at the showrooms of several music publishers. The quality can differ to an astonishing extent. See the warnings on pages 80–81, and be prepared to pay for the most expensive sort that is available.

Ink for music-copying should be of a 'special black' quality: waterproof, and suitable for photographic reproduction.

Nibs can cause a lot of trouble. Buy single 'reservoir' nibs of different shapes and sizes, and try them out on minims, crotchets, quavers, and slurs while you are still in the shop, before deciding which to order.

Rulers should be long enough to stretch from the top stave to the bottom of a sheet of manuscript paper. Transparent rulers can be helpful. Professional copyists often use T squares and architects' rulers that move from side to side on rollers.

Pencils should be of the best quality for drawing, and soft enough to rub out easily.

Rubbers must also be of the best quality, particularly if you are rubbing out other conductors' expression marks on hired copies of printed music: an obstinate rubber can wear holes in the paper.

Adhesive mending tape should be transparent, waterproof, and with a matt surface.

Folding 'blackboards' that roll up are obtainable from large music shops which supply teaching equipment to schools.

Duplicating and photocopying firms will send details of what they charge for their work. If possible, find a firm that has some experience in reproducing music: small blemishes that would be harmless on a duplicated typescript can cause trouble if they appear between the lines of the staves.

Music stands can be a problem. The cheapest are the 'stacking' music stands made of tubular steel, but they are little use for conducting, because even when the height is adjustable, the angle of the desk remains fixed. A conductor's stand has to be fully adjustable, and it has to be large enough and strong enough to support a full score. This means that it will be expensive to buy. But if you are going to do a good deal of conducting with an orchestra, it will be worth the money that is spent on it.

ADDRESSES OF MUSIC PUBLISHERS

Boosey & Hawkes Music Publishers Ltd.
   Showroom at 295 Regent Street, London, W.1
   Catalogues from The Hyde, Edgware Road, London, N.W.9
Curwen-Faber (available from Faber Music Ltd.)
Curwen-Roberton (available from Roberton Publications)
J. & W. Chester Ltd.
   Eagle Court, London, E.C.1
Faber Music Ltd.
   38 Russell Square, London, W.C.1
Galliard Ltd. (formerly Augener)
   Publishing Services Partnership, 82 High Road, East Finchley, London, N.2.

Novello & Company Ltd.
  Showroom at 27/28 Soho Square, London, W.1
  Catalogues from Borough Green, Sevenoaks, Kent
Oxford University Press
  Music Department, 44 Conduit Street, London, W.1
Roberton Publications
  The Windmill, Wendover, Aylesbury, Bucks.
Schott & Co. Ltd.
  48 Great Marlborough Street, London, W.1
Stainer and Bell Ltd.
  Publishing Services Partnership, 82 High Road, East Finchley, London,
  N.2.

MUSIC PUBLISHERS IN AMERICA
Belwin-Mills Publishing Corporation
  16 West Sixty-first St., New York, N.Y. 10023
Boosey and Hawkes Inc.
  30 West Fifty-seventh St., New York, N.Y. 10019
Carl Fischer Inc.
  62 Cooper Square, New York, N.Y. 10003
Galaxy Music Corporation
  2121 Broadway, New York, N.Y. 10023
E. B. Marks Music Corporation
  136 West Fifty-second St., New York, N.Y. 10019
MCA Music
  445 Park Avenue, New York, N.Y. 10022
Oxford University Press Inc.
  200 Madison Avenue, New York, N.Y. 10116
C. F. Peters Corporation
  373 Park Avenue South, New York, N.Y. 10016
Theodore Presser Corporation
  Presser Place, Bryn Mawr, Philadelphia 19010
G. Schirmer Inc.
  609 Fifth Avenue, New York, N.Y. 10017

ADDRESSES OF ORGANIZATIONS
British Federation of Music Festivals
  106 Gloucester Place, London, W.1

English Folk Dance and Song Society
  Cecil Sharp House, 2 Regent's Park Road, London, N.W.1
The Music Teachers' Association
  106 Gloucester Place, London, W.1
National Association of Choirs
  48 Crossefield Road, Cheadle Hulme, Cheadle, Cheshire
National Council of Social Service
  (The Standing Conference for Amateur Music), 26 Bedford Square,
    London, W.C.1
National Federation of Music Societies
  29 Exhibition Road, South Kensington, London, S.W.7
National Federation of Women's Institutes
  39 Eccleston Street, London, S.W.1
Performing Right Society
  29–33 Berners Street, London, W.1
Rural Music Schools Association
  Little Benslow Hills, Hitchin, Hertfordshire
Workers' Music Association
  236 Westbourne Park Road, London, W.11

ORGANIZATIONS IN AMERICA

American Choral Directors Association
  Wisconsin State University, Eau Claire, Wisconsin 54701
American Federation of Musicians
  641 Lexington Avenue, New York, N.Y. 10022
American Guild of Musical Artists
  1841 Broadway, New York, N.Y. 10023
American Music Center
  2109 Broadway, New York, N.Y. 10023
American Society of Composers, Authors, and Publishers
  1 Lincoln Plaza, New York, N.Y. 10023
Broadcast Music Inc.
  589 Fifth Avenue, New York, N.Y. 10017
Music Educators National Conference
  1201 Sixteenth St., N.W., Washington, D.C. 20036
Music Publishers' Association of the United States
  609 Fifth Avenue, New York, N.Y. 10017

Alphabetical list of first lines of music examples

Index

In this short Index, only the page-number on which the main references occur is mentioned. (See also the detailed paragraph headings on pages v to x.)

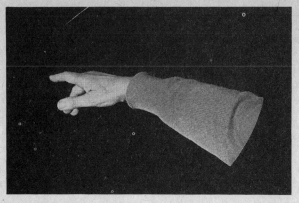

(a) The pointing forefinger as an alternative to a stick

(b) Practising a preparatory upbeat

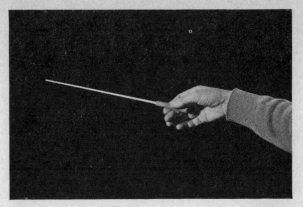

(c) Learning to hold the stick with a relaxed hand before conducting

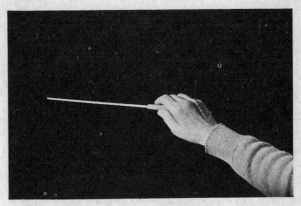

(d) Using the stick as an extension of the hand and arm